To Sue ~

May these short glimpses of life bring you something good to think about, as you each recover. As we cooperate with God's plan for our lives we always win!

Blessings,
Kay
2023

She Thinks!

A Collection of True Stories to Bring You Peace and Joy

K.L. LYONS

WESTBOW
PRESS®
A DIVISION OF THOMAS NELSON
& ZONDERVAN

WestBow Press books may be ordered through booksellers or by contacting:

WestBow Press
A Division of Thomas Nelson & Zondervan
1663 Liberty Drive
Bloomington, IN 47403
www.westbowpress.com
1 (866) 928-1240

ISBN: 978-1-4908-9160-6 (sc)
ISBN: 978-1-4908-9161-3 (hc)
ISBN: 978-1-4908-9216-0 (e)

Print information available on the last page.

WestBow Press rev. date: 10/05/2015

Contents

Dedication

I dedicate this book to the one woman who has shown me the importance of living my life, to the fullest, on this earth and that is my Mom. Agnes Eileen Rae York.

It is very difficult to name one single person in my life who has influenced me more, as there are so many who are important to me: My dear husband, Fred, and our awesome children; Colleen and Bob, Dan and Ruth, Mike and Sonia, Patrick and Michelle. I include in this my unbelievably smart, gorgeous, charming, and graceful grandchildren and great grandchildren, who each take after their grandparents, of course! I wish to remember my sisters and brothers, and all of my wonderful friends. All of these people have their handprint on my writing as it is they who have inspired, encouraged, and helped me along the way of my journey and thus far through life. They have spoken to me or shown me the importance of God, whether intentionally or unknowingly. To all I say; thank you and I love you.

Foreword

What are you thinking? Do you look forward to getting up each morning? Is today going to be fun, productive, or wearisome or worse? Would you like to walk out each day with joy and a zest for living? Sound impossible? It's not!

"There's always something!" as the late television comedian and philosopher, Gilda Radner has said. No one is immune to difficulty, small or huge, in this life. There are so many things that bring anxiety and worry: finances, family, sickness, pain, our country, even death and on and on and on. Such events we all share. Such occurrences, and how to cope with them, are what this book is all about.

Wondering and wandering all over the page; I asked myself what you might really want to know. Yes, we share these events. How does one think good thoughts at the same time that he/she is having trouble? Is there really a silver lining to the dark clouds? No matter what you are currently facing, happy thoughts can be yours. You can face each day with a smile. Sound impossible? It's not!

So much happens in life. Most seems beyond one's control. Much is, in fact, out of one's control. However there is one thing that is not, one very important thing. That is our thoughts. No one, truly no one, has control over your thoughts, except you!

"I am the master of my fate. I am the captain of my soul." These words were written by a well-renowned English poet of yesteryear, in his poem *Invictus*. Is he right? Can you agree? Are you the master of your fate, the captain of your soul?

Your thoughts give rise to your feelings, sad or glad, anxious or awesome. Then these emotions motivate you. They give words to your mouth and spark to your will. What you think about is what you talk about. Your words reflect your thoughts. In turn, what you talk about is what you get. What you (and I) think about is what your (and my) life *was, is and will become.*

How does this happen? How do yours and my thoughts and words affect our lives, our destiny? As Calvin and Hobbes say, "Don't just sit there, do *nothing!*" For in reality, even though it appears that you are accomplishing nothing; your life is being planned out by your thoughts. Strange as it may sound, even with drastic difficulty, our reactions are so much more important than the actual event. Each one of us can truly become the master of his/her fate and the captain of his/her ship. An amazing realization! So very powerful!

This is a powerful truth to recognize. Thoughts and words create a map toward one's destiny. This is true, whether man, woman or child. Once this truth is really understood; this road can be followed or changed to reach one's destiny. So I ask you again, "What kind of morning do you want to start each day? What kind of life do you want? What are you thinking about? What words are you speaking?"

There is a definite cause and effect to these questions. Recent medical and sociological research supports this truth. It is documented scientifically in numerous publications. What doctors and brain research scientists are finding out about how one can reprogram his/her brain to view trials and tragedy in a new way is very interesting. Even if you have experienced terrible or horrific happenings in your past or present; you can change your take on such events. As you take charge of your thoughts; changes in your life occur. Coincidentally, this truth is also biblical.

May the message in these stories found on the following pages repeatedly give you food for thought as you read all or only the pages that appeal to you. Re-read sections as you are prompted by your thoughts and feelings. These stories contain the "how" to move on, to heal, to greet each day the way you desire. You can create the life you want.

She Thinks is divided in four parts. Start at the beginning or turn to the section you are most interested in today. The four sections are:

I.   Spring: A Time of Renewal and Healing.

II. Summer: A Time of the Beauty of Full Blossoming of Flowers and Friends.

III. Autumn: A Time of the Glorious Colors of Our Country.

IV. Winter: a Time of Special Beauty to Celebrate Death.

Ponder on what you are thinking about, talking about; and how these thoughts and words determine your days and destiny. Read on and enjoy.

> "Earth is crammed with heaven
> And every common bush alive with God.
> But only he who sees takes off his shoes;
> The rest sit around and pluck blackberries."
>
> *Elizabeth Barrett Browning*

PART I:

Spring: A Time of Renewal and Healing

Spring Magic

She wants to capture this instant…this magic.
When her soul feels tired;
but her heart does not.
She's like the sprouting crocus –
fresh and green and reaching
for the warmth, the sun.

Monet

The painting takes her there;
What he did with color and light.
Not just an instrument,
Not just a receiver.
He captured the time so right;
the moment, the hour.
She wants to see more.

She wants to feel more.
She wants to be more.
She asks, "where? when? how?"
She hears the answer:
"In the creation of nature."

Rebirth

The first peep of green from the black soil,
Warm sun on her back and in her eyes,
A squirrel chattering,
A bird peck-pecking;
Far off a child's laughter is heard.
The kite flying higher and higher into the clouds,
The smell of rain coming soon,
Rebirths, renewal, realize the miracle of spring.

"…those who hope in the Lord will renew
their strength."

-the NIV Bible, Isaiah 40:31

She awakes each morning with varying thoughts swirling in her mind, often just about her plans for the day. It's quiet now in her home, so different from when she was growing up. She was raised in a traditional large family: lots of kids, brothers and sisters both, lots of noise, lots of food, and lots of fun. She remembers skipping through life in the security of being loved. She continues to do so. She loved being a child in so many different ways. She has so many fond memories. Perhaps she has let go of any, not so fond. The blind faith that she's been gifted with turns all each day into glorious fun. She has been on a long journey with a little stumbling along the way; but always getting up, brushing off and starting over. This habit was taught to her in watching her parents. She thanks her God for all the encouragement He has given her to help her, both through His written word and through all the people in her life. Her spiritual development and growth has come from many, but mostly from her quiet time with Him. This is what she focuses on each morning.

Morning Thoughts

Strong winds blowing outside the shield of windows toss the branches mightily. The snow is leaving drip by drip, rivulet by rivulet, down the embankment to quench the thirst of the hiding woodland ferns. One can hear the wind's fierceness against the building. All outside huddle against the wind, as shoulders are hunched to walk out the day's agenda. Thoughts are not on spring right now; but rather on getting in out of the wind and cold.

Wait, the cold bluster is stopping. A ray of spring warmth is coming. This she knows from experience, year after year after year.

May the wind of wisdom clear away any confusion in the minds and hearts of self and loved ones today. May the perfect, immeasurable, unstoppable Love lead all thoughts, emotions, words, and decisions made.

As a child, a morning prayer was learned each day. As a sometimes doubting teen, it may have been skipped over. As a busy young mother; it was uttered to the bonging of the clock, the clamor of children's voices, phones buzzing, books misplaced. As a grandmother, kneeling and praying for the generations, an hour is spent in petition for protection. The Voice of Wisdom can be missed among the clamor of life sometimes, of kitchen, of traffic, of school rooms, of meetings, of busy schedules. But..... listen.

The day's light breaks through quietly and streams in the window. The reminder of the brightness of the glory of God as seen in the face of Jesus Christ, as thanks are offered. Gratitude is spoken for the sun breaking through; to feel the warmth, to relax the shoulders. The sound of the mourning dove breaks the silence. Hope for the greenness of the land returns. He brings new grace and mercy every morning. This is just as true as the coming of spring each year that she has witnessed for many years. Without grasping this truth, concern, dismay and depression could run as quickly as the water running from the melting snow pile. She abides in this knowledge. She wants to speak and act in love like His today. She wants to find the end of herself. She wants to find her will to be His will. He gives her strength to face the day. He gives her joy to walk out the day; to help her to trust. She trusted Him for her healing, over the past years. His peace covered her through His Word in her spirit. His strength is hers now. Prayer makes her home a holy place each morning. Prayer makes her day a holy day. She considers an important thought:

> "All we have to decide is what to do with the time that is given us."

-JRR Tolkien

She watches the last hurrah of winter giving way to spring; looking for something a little deeper than the whiteness of the snow. She wants to walk in it like a child, to kick the crustiness away. Such crustiness in her mind needs to be broken up, as well. She asks for help, the insight from His Wisdom as to how to do so.

The Peaceful Whiteness Returns

After the rain washes all the rooftops, the streets shine with sheets of water. Grass pokes through the gray stiffness of the still frozen earth. All the evergreens, soon to show their true color, are dehiscent again. Buds are almost visible on the bare, woody branches of the old oak tree. Then in the quiet of the dark night, a heavy snow falls. Everything is white. Morning sun streams through the brightness, almost blinding. In this one short day the temperature has changed the vista dramatically. The old and pale and tired becomes reborn into beauty. Worn ruts are covered, even deep mucky ones

The heart and soul often mirrors this change from sin and sadness to heightened freedom and forgiveness. So similar is the scene without that matches the one within. Stumbling often, even falling from grace through blackness; then a bright light of repentance and replenishment. Thanksgiving is given for new mercies offered every day. Tears and tares of the heart are cleansed. Peace and whiteness are here. So simple, just for asking, they are given; even just by agreeing to receive them.

> "It matters not so much *what* happens to one in life; but rather how one *reacts* to what happens.
>
> –*Aldus Huxley, quote paraphrased by Author*

"Keep putting into practice all you have learned from me (the Holy Spirit) and heard from me (the Holy Spirit) and saw me (the Holy Spirit) doing, and the God of peace will be with you."

-The NLT Bible, Philippians 4:9
Parenthesis emphasis by the author

"Show me the path where I should walk, oh Lord. Point out the right road for me to follow."

-the NLT Bible, Psalm 25:4

She received the news about the dreaded disease attacking a very close friend. This message fills her with anxiety; worry about what the future holds for this dear person. As a child, she didn't, couldn't understand from where this sickness came. She perseveres, not by her own strength, but as a child holding the hand of one who loves her and leads her; that guides her on the journey of life. She releases the source of sickness and pain to often be, not only one's personal choices regarding lifestyle; but often, the snares of the one who comes to steal, kill, and destroy.

Her Friend Is Sick

She woke early in the dawn.
The room was gray.
Her friend was sick.
She tossed.
She turned.
She prayed.
She slept awhile longer, fitfully.
The bright sun awoke her again.
The sparkling filtered
Through the leaves.
The room was golden.
Hope had come.
Hope had come through His Word.
Hope remains forever.

"Jesus said I will come and heal him. ... He healed them all."

-the NLT Bible, Matthew 8:7, 16

The fear that can haunt the soul of the cancer survivor is common. It can become debilitating if left unchecked. She, herself, received this diagnosis. She overcame stage IV cancer twice within 15 years. There was fear. There was anxiety. There was pain. Finally there was victory, in Him. In the hope of helping someone else, this is her story of finally overcoming this irrational feeling of...

Fighting Fear

Is *anything* wrong with the glorious change of seasons in the Midwest? She tearfully says good-by to one. She joyfully sings hello to another with its warmth of lighted windows in the early dusk. Green sprouts bring the hope of summer's beatific blooms. Summer flowers fill the air with sweetness as the sun beats down. The beautiful tall oak and maple trees cascading a rainbow down the hill with their varying colors are breathtaking. Autumn walks the woods and turns the painted trees over to the snowy peace of winter whiteness. Each season so unique it is difficult to pick a favorite. Yet woven into all this beauty of changing seasons; there is an ugliness stalking her. As she feels sadness in each leaving; the joyful anticipation of the next to appear is constant. However there is always a darkness that doesn't flee. It stays with her. It seems to be constantly following her, coloring the landscape with grayness. It is this paranoia of succumbing to cancer again. Not the physical, but the emotional impact: the dreadful fear of the disease returning. Darkness dims the golden colors of each new season for her. Frightening thoughts come into her head. How does she fight the fear that cancer leaves in its' aftermath? How to have true joyful anticipation, instead of a facsimile, with the astounding newness as the calendar turns, month by month? Three ugly experiences have left her with this fear; the fear that is known well to the cancer survivor. Often, this fear is trying to befriend the loved ones of the over-comer. Even those, whose body has never betrayed them, this way, are familiar with the anxiety of unexplained weight loss, a weird pain felt, a strange lump appearing. One's body, experiencing puzzling changes, brings worry.

She has overcome cancer twice. Both times, stage 4 which spread to other parts of her body. Sandwiched in between these two attacks, a rare blood disorder threatened her life. These three threatening events each occurred in the time of one season leaving, and welcoming another. Three different segue that were tinged with sadness. These experiences left her with a growing anxiety. It came often, in the cooling evening, along with the smell of leaves burning. In the late afternoon snowfall or the early spring rain, even the summer evening walk-each a time of reflection. What was she thinking about? She has now come to believe that these thoughts worked and weakened her immune system enough to let a single cancer cell become way too powerful!

Only recently has triumph come. Only recently, the frightening spirit of blackness has been stopped. This is her story of how this dread began and how it grew into something much too massive.

It's a beautiful warm, sunny Sunday afternoon. Walking into the family room with a cup of coffee in her hand; she glances out the window at the gorgeous colors. She revels in the moment in the beauty of the landscape dressed in unimaginable brightness.

Darkness slices through the sunshine; as she falls. Coffee splashes everywhere on the white carpet. Like a spindly leg of a dainty tea table overburdened with weight, her slim body goes limp as her legs refuse to keep her standing. She watches in puzzlement as her thigh bulges and then recedes. She remembers her right leg had been aching for about a month. She heard the crack of the femur bone. The sound was that of a really good golf ball hit. A few weeks previously she had discovered a strange bump on the back of her head. She sloughed it off thinking she probably banged her head on something. Of all the things to happen that day, she counted the worst to be in the emergency room, when they cut off her favorite pair of sweats! Yikes – never to be worn again! Or so she thought. She didn't know yet about the uninvited intruder invading her body and that it was beginning to set up residence in her spirit.

At first, the doctors thought it was CUO: cancer of undetermined origin. The words of a well-meaning but inexperienced intern frightened her. "Even at autopsy time, we can't say where the cancer originated. It's very hard to treat. Chemotherapy becomes a shotgun approach." She heard this before even an "official" diagnosis or cause for the broken leg was given. She politely thanked him. Mentally she screamed, "Get out of this room! I don't want to think about my autopsy! I want to think about living to see my grandkids." Four or five days passed; until the biopsy report came back. It was not CUO. But, the seed of fear had now been born. Her anxiety watered the seed with frightening thoughts. What if…what if? What if it can't be treated? What if the treatment doesn't work? What if there was too much pain in her future?

Finally, the diagnosis came under the pathologist's signature: cancer of the lymph system. It is advanced, stage four lymphoma. It had spread to her kidneys, skull, and femur, the large bone inside her thigh. Was she going to die? Was she not going to live to see her grandchildren? Was her life here on earth soon to be over? Is this the last time she will see the painting of the seasons change? Despair gripped her. It choked her. She tried to fight these negative thoughts, with family, with friends, with prayer. It worked somewhat for a time. She felt the healing hand of God.

As Matt Redman sings in his recording of *I Need You Now*. "On this thirsty desert ground, in a dry and barren land, I bow down… You will call and I will come…I need you now."

The wonder of chemotherapy drugs was experienced. After eight rounds, she was cancer free. An experimental bone marrow transplant was recommended. Her own bone marrow was used. It changed the likelihood of relapse significantly down from 80% to 20%. It also fertilized her growing fear as she reflected upon the likelihood of the 20%, chance of relapse. After the months of recovering from the high dose chemotherapy given in the transplant; she was back on her way to health. As the time of chemicals drew further away; busy schedules, work, and fun times became her life again.

It doesn't take long to forget the pain but the fear was always lurking in the shadows. Lurking, lurking, lurking…the "C" word set up residence in more dark corners of her mind. Even though, she was smiling and laughing on the outside; often she was trying to ignore the fear growing inside, pretending that it wasn't there.

Every time the seasons changed, the different smells and sights brought the memory of her changing health forward in her mind to ponder. She allowed it to take up the valuable "real estate" of her mind. The dread became alive again. It took on a life of its own. It grew. The fear of cancer returning is irrational. It is without medical cause. But, it becomes all consuming of her thoughts and emotions. Never realizing, that she had the power to kill it; it followed her like an evil spirit into the grocery store, into the book store, into church, into her children's school, into her friend's home, into her bedroom at night. It was always, always there. She tried to ignore it, but was not successful.

A few years later, after her return to work, she is very tired as she walks down the long corridor at school to check her mail box.

She just collapses on the chair in the office for a few minutes. She is familiar again with that beloved smell of school: the odor of white boards, markers, chalk, lunch bags, and books. This is a smell beloved only by a teacher! She is truly exhausted and wonders why. Her hands look yellowish. Her students had questioned her this afternoon, "Why are you sitting down so much? Don't you feel good? Are you sick?" She usually didn't ever sit down while teaching. Their innocent questions give more fuel to the fear. What is going on? Is it cancer again? Even though, she was going through her days apparently "normal". The fear was always, always there; waiting to jump, wanting to grow and devour any joy.

The black shadow overtakes her. She is very ill. Off to the hospital again. This time it is not cancer. But it is, in some ways, even more serious: acute idiopathic hemolytic anemia. These are million dollar doctor words. They put a name on what was happening to her. The cause is unknown – maybe a virus? Her blood was disappearing, a truly life-threatening condition. Within a couple of days, a third of her blood was gone! Her red blood count is down to five when normal is around 14. Her veins are starting to collapse. Her urine is black, at the time of the first transfusion. She is having trouble breathing. She lays there awake the rest of the night, wondering. What is it? What is going on? She prays. That's all she knows to do. She is desperate.

Another well-meaning, but inexperienced doctor came to tell her that if her count goes down anymore, she will be transferred to another floor. This doctor notes that "it would be foolish to pound on your chest because you will be loopy by then." Her response: "that's not going to happen." The doctor warns that no one knows what's going to happen. The doctor was trying to ask if she wanted artificial methods used to prolong her life. Of course her heart almost stopped in fright right then. Wasn't there a less frightening way to ask?

Finally, after consultations between the hospital, the near-by university, and the American Red Cross doctors, a transfusion of white platelets helps. She waits for her blood count to go up towards normal. It climbs very, very slowly with the assistance of a powerful steroid. It takes months of exhaustion. She watches the sunlight diffused through the window shades in her bedroom.

Approximately seven months later, her count is hovering near normal. Her red-blood-eating spleen has settled down. She tearfully decides to retire. She cries because she adores her second graders. But often more than a few of them were coughing, sneezing kiddos. The sad decision is made to leave the school environment because she doesn't need another weird virus attacking her already compromised immune system. This decision is made out of fear. It is not a medical recommendation. She is now allowing the dark dread to rule her life, actually affecting her destiny. Her thought life was doing its' damage.

By the following summer she is pretty much back to her normal productive life. The bad dream is over! Yay! Retirement and a full life are on the horizon. Or so *She Thinks*! Once again as the next season comes, so does change. This new season is laced with a black lining. The giant fear is always hovering, and ready to pounce! She cannot rid herself of it, once and for all!

Throughout these times, she does a great job of hiding this fear. Only she knows what's going on in her darker thoughts. They come at varying times of the day and night, never quite giving her peace; but rather stealing it from her. She goes on; continues planning life.

A few years later, she and her husband are moving, after retirement, to a new home, just built. Schlepping boxes around, climbing up and down, packing glassware, heavy dishes, fills the days. Is this increased activity causing the back pain she feels? Or is it something else? Could it be something worse? Her aching is getting worse. It's waking her up at night. The fear of cancer starts to loom larger and larger. In the darkness of her sleepless nights, she worries. The fear comes back. It is real. It is settling in, expanding.

CT scans confirm that it is the threatening disease again: Lymphoma, advanced, stage four. It is in her liver, kidneys, pancreas, and lymph nodes. The doctor puts the film up on the bright light. She sees so many tumors in her liver, too many to count. She is becoming blinded. "Oh no, no, no! How? How can this be, it's been so many years?" Thirteen years later! She really thought she was home free after five years: the magical number – cure achieved, right? Wrong! She walks out of the doctor's office on automatic pilot. She is in shock. How does she even drive home? As she walked into the kitchen, devastated, she stumbles into the arms of her husband and starts sobbing. "It's back. The cancer's back!" Crying and weeping filled the next week. Breaking down into tears, she told her now grown children, her brothers, sisters and friends. Another beautiful season turned to soggy, mossy clouds of blackness following her around. This vile enemy is winning!

After another eight rounds of chemo with all the same side effects; and same long recuperation period, she is again, cancer free. She is living a full life – except as each season change calls forth the sneaking enemy of fear. The dismay turns to terror. Will it be like this throughout all of her life? Will she ever have a beautiful harvest time full of joy? Will she ever enjoy the bright sunshine of springtime instead of the darkness blinding her in this hidden fear? Can she ever rid herself of this increasing paranoia? She has had cancer twice. She has had the weird uncontrollable anemia. What is going to happen this year? She shudders with apprehension. What malevolence lies in wait for her?

Early this summer, she was feeling tired, achy, and feverish. "A relapse can come on that way, but not usually," was the comment made by her oncologist at the yearly check up. That's all she needed to hear to give fuel to the fire! By August, the mental turmoil is overcoming all hope of calm. Is she getting really sick again?" Her thinking goes wild.

Every time there's a new pain, or ache, or she just feels run down with a cold, her thoughts run to "What if it's cancer again?" This fear stalks her like the night darkness. It's her worst nightmare; walking beside her all of her waking hours. The gray mornings turn to dark purple to black evening as far-reaching fear enters her thoughts. It intrudes on her sleep in the middle of the night. She curses it!

She has to find a way to fight. Maybe, just maybe… there is a way. Then there comes a momentous change as she realizes something. Through prayer, research, healing classes and God-given insight, understanding and peace came. The Holy Spirit helps her to do some deep soul searching about harboring this fear.

As her family prayed with her the evening of the second diagnosis, her son cites a prayer about God having plans for her future, good plans, not to harm her. She grabs onto this truth. When a pastor prays with her husband and self; the pastor asked her how long she wanted to live. Through tears, she answered at least until she turns 95, more than some thirty years hence.

Always in prayer with insight given her by the Holy Spirit; she begins to discover how to rid herself of this dark fear. The only way she can pull herself out of the pit of worry and self-pity is not a chocolate bar or watching a funny movie; although sometimes this seems to help. Finally deep down, she realizes that she can be free. She comes to know where to find help. She knows she can depend on Him. The battle is in her head; not her body. Her weapons of war are her thoughts. She designs her rehab plan for her soul, her mind. She searches Scripture. With the dreadful fright of cancer returning; she takes hold of every negative thought. She kills each one. She stomps the life out of it. This is her mind choice. It doesn't matter what she's feeling. *Either she believes His Word that she is healed or she does not. Either she lets herself doubt or she does not.* It is a choice. She decides, down deep, that she really does want to live and not die, to declare the works of her God!

After much praying, pondering, and putting her pencil to paper in her journal; she has come to the *personal insight that she became well because with the unlimited grace of God*; she thought herself *well*. That is why she felt such great need to find a way to stop the toxicity of her fright. She cannot answer why this hasn't worked for others. She would never even attempt it. It may be error in her thinking. Or it may be simple lack of knowledge on the part of a suffering person or even the battle fatigue and weariness of living in this tainted world. She knows that it is not lack of faith; as the Book tells her that faith as tiny as mustard seed is enough. That little seed becomes huge, in the hands of God. Most likely the answer of why she was healed and not someone else won't be answered this side of heaven.

She discovers finally the now seemingly simple battle strategy of positive thoughts. She replaces every bad thought with a picture that makes her smile. She says no to all anxious thoughts. There is no room for them in her head! The choice *is* hers to believe. Her mind choice, her thinking, determines what she feels; *not vice versa!* When she awakes at night with anxious thoughts, knocking at the door of her mind and emotions, with scary thoughts trying to enter; what does she do? She forces worry and anxiety out with praises for God. She repeats His healing promises to herself over and over and over. She had printed His healing promises and placed them all around her home: near the phone, in the kitchen, taped to the bathroom wall. Through repetition, the belief finally becomes part of her spirit as it travels from her words to her mind to her heart! It is so simple that she asks herself why she let this fear grow so huge, so controlling of her in the past. Why did she let this paranoia use a black crayon to outline so many beautiful seasons with dark slashes?

She found that there is a real way to overcome this demon. The rehab plan for her thinking works. Her spirit, the Spirit of Christ within her takes charge. Her body has to line with the Truth. There is no choice. Something is happening within her. She sees herself crunching through the dry leaves in the fall. They crack and scatter as she walks. They blow away. In the winter, she turns her face up to watch the snowflakes float down. Every branch is covered with white pureness. Spring brings her a picture in her mind of flowers, an abundance of color, riotous in their glory. She sees herself waking barefoot in the grass, inhaling nature's perfume. Then fall arrives again. So what now? Victory! She is dancing and twirling in the falling russet leaves. She is truly joyful again! She raises her hands in thanksgiving for this insight given her by the Holy Spirit of Jesus! The sequence of the seasons is no longer dreaded. It is totally enjoyed. The emotional and spiritual scars of cancer are gone simply because she thinks them gone. She speaks them gone; by speaking His word. Really!

She remembers a nurse at the hospital at the time of her first diagnosis. The nurse was native born from a country in the Eastern hemisphere. When the quiet mannered nurse was diagnosed with cancer; she chose not to have treatment. She simply went about her daily work in confidence. She was not totally healthy, but she refused to worry. Therefore, toxic thoughts had no power within her. Was this a miracle? Maybe not? In a sense every healing is a miracle. But maybe this nurse knew the secret key to healing. Doctors and medicine and treatment are critical components. But they cannot do it alone. Are these beliefs yet additional incidences showing the power of positive thinking in healing? Of course prayer is overwhelmingly the most important factor. Of what value is thinking good, pleasant thoughts in the healing process, becomes the question.

She truly doesn't understand it all; but comfort covers her like a warm blanket on a frosty autumn night. She is now free to enjoy this beautiful season. After taking control of her thinking, she is free from the fear of succumbing to cancer ever again. She is free from the emotional and spiritual scars which have caused numbing doubts in the past. They no longer exist. Every morning as the sun awakens her, she is amazed and delighted. Her joyful hope stretches unending through the seasons of her life now. It is boundless. Her faith in Him causes the autumn sunshine, the blinding whiteness of snow, the fresh greenness of spring, and the colorful summer blooms, to never stop. The golden red foliage of the trees shimmers in the morning sun. It is glorious; echoing the jewel colored waves of peace in her heart. Everyday she dances in the silver and gold. Everyday she raises her hands in thankful praise to the artist who paints the beauty of the universe. Never to feel or think of this one terror again, only has her continual gratitude remained. She knows she could not have done this alone. Nor can she keep the terror from resurrecting itself without the strength given her by God each day.

If the blackness tries to re-enter, she strikes with the Truth, which tells of her faith in her Healer:

> "We are human, but we don't wage war with human plans, we use God's mighty weapons, mere worldly weapons, to knock down the devil's strongholds. With these weapons we break down every proud argument that keeps us from knowing God. With these weapons, we conquer these rebellious ideas and teach our minds to obey our Christ."

> *-The NLT Bible, 2 Corinthians 10:4*

She calls this to mind continually as she laughs off the doubts that try to gain entrance each time she has an ache or pain. She feels again the freedom of a child, skipping down the path, looking forward to the future to find her destiny.

Just a little bit of confused anxiety enters her; as making a decision presents difficulty. She knows where it is easier for her to listen for the answer. Like a child she runs to her Father to ease the perplexity in her soul. She has learned that wisdom is hers for the asking.

The Little Garden: A Meeting Place

Upon waking in the early morning, she asked a question of her God. She is seeking wisdom. She is drawn to her garden. It is such a tiny garden. On the path sits a single lone bench on which to rest, to stop, to listen to the birds calling She sits in her garden. The sunlight is so bright. A bee buzzes by. The ice in her glass of water melts. Her face is getting hot as the sun comes through the holes in her silly straw hat. She notices that the spring forget-me-nots are starting to wilt. The pansies smell so sweet. They move slightly in the soft breeze. She waits.

While she waits her mind wonders to a friend who is going through a difficult time. She looks at the stone in her garden that says, "Friends share love". She sends a quick encouraging prayer toward heaven. She wants to go in and bake cookies for her friend. But she stays for a while longer. Her eyes close against the sun. Her elbow slips down off the arm of the bench. It must be time to go in. But she doesn't. Why is she hesitating? What is she waiting for? Who is she waiting for? It's just that she doesn't want to leave this place where peace is permeating her being. He has met her here. He has answered her. This knowledge stills the uneasiness. Her answer comes to mind as she prays: to continue, to move forward. It is settled in her spirit and soul. She goes freely to the kitchen to bake her favorite chocolate chunk cookies.

> "If a man lacks wisdom, let him ask God, who gives freely of all good things. But when he asks, let him doubt not..."

-the NIV Bible, James 1:5

She awoke one morning, while under the medical treatment for cancer and heard in her mind and in her heart....

How to Heal

She's learned how to heal;
It comes from the soul, from that deep quiet place.
She can go there anytime.
He's there...the Spirit of God within her;
To take her hand and heart and make her well.
Just ask,
Then be still and listen;
She waits for the peace and joy of Healing to enter her spirit.

"Go in peace, daughter... your faith has made thee well".

-the NIV Bible, Matthew 9:22
(Paraphrased by author)

She considers the spiritual battle occurring in the unseen as she busies herself with the ordinary tasks of her day. She doesn't want to lose her way; to follow the path that will take her down the road of prodding slowly, heavy laden. Her habit is skipping lightly and laughing through her days as a child would do. There are times when she must focus totally on His promises. Almost everyday, she meets a battle of the spirits of good and evil. She fights. She wins, only with His strength.

When She Is Weak

She needs to talk with Him. She needs to go to that special place, that holy place, and knock on the door where she can see her God. He opens it and bids her in. He touches her shoulder and her face gently. She needs His strength, oh Lord, today. She wants to be one with Him in spirit and mind and will. She does not want to be discouraged, or wondering. She fidgets, and fusses, and frets. She worries. She hurts. She wants to bless Him. She wants to hear Him say that she, His child, is blessed. She pleads His strength, and His joy.

What do you want of her, Lord? She wants to be filled with gratitude to her God for listening and answering. She can be. She is. She is thankful that she knows Him and that she can hear His Spirit speak to her; and that she can meet Him.

She puts on her armor of faith. She raises the shield and sword of His word. No weapon formed against her shall ever succeed. Greater is He, who is in her, than he who is in the world. She is your chosen, your beloved daughter, your princess. She trusts her God.

Is this what Her God wants of her? She never, ever wants to be out of His grace. She never shall. He has unlimited grace and new mercy for her everyday. Let her hear and truly know His word, His will. Give her courage. She can go to this special place within herself to talk with Him to see His face smiling at her. She thanks Him for always being there, to help her when she falters. Forgive her, Lord, for not trusting her future totally to Him.

> "Put on the full armor of God so that you can take your stand against the devil's schemes. For our struggle is not against flesh and blood but against the rulers, the authorities, and the powers of the dark world and against the spiritual forces of evil in the heavenly realms. Therefore put on the full armor of God so that when the day of evil comes you will be able to stand your ground. And after you have done everything, stand firm then, with the belt of truth buckled round your waist, with the breast-plate of righteousness in place and with your feet fitted with the readiness that comes from the gospel of peace. In addition to all of this, take up the shield of faith with which you can extinguish all the flaming arrows of the evil one. Take the helmet of salvation and the sword of the spirit, which is the word of God and pray... "

-The NIV Bible, Ephesians 6:10-17

She continues on her journey. She is thinking happy thoughts.

As her life's partner faces a test to identify a possible malignancy, the ugliness raises its' head again. Her imagination can run away with her emotions; even as her emotions lead her thoughts. Worry enters her soul as…

Fear Slices through Her Heart

There is a word that strikes fear into every heart. That word is "cancer". Those who have received the diagnosis, those with the well-known symptoms but yet undiagnosed, those with strange discomfort, all feel anxiety about this word. Some experiences have even led her and others to grow to hate the word, signifying pain, disfigurement, even death.

Now, fear slices through her heart like a razor sharp knife slicing through her favorite chocolate mousse pie. Almost all of the time, her heart is as full and content as her stomach, like the happy emotional state that comes after she savors one of these sweet treats; as the endorphins are released. Now at biopsy time, a whisper comes: "What if…..? What if it's the dreaded C word? What if the tomorrow holds pain and sickness and even possibly death for her beloved?" She tells herself to focus on the truth of her Healer's word instead of worry and anxiety and all of the varied horridness that may happen tomorrow or in the future. She fights fear, the uninvited visitor.

"How silly," she tells herself. "He could die on his way to the golf course, right?" Oh where is she going in her mind? She admonishes herself, "Get a hold girl!" She casts out such thoughts quickly because she knows her Christ as Healer. How? She knows, first of all, from the truth spoken in His Word. She also knows from her own personal experiences of overcoming cancer. She has come to know that Jesus took all diseases in the stripes on His back as He was beaten. Her wayward thinking diverting her must halt!

> "Verily I say unto you, that whosoever shall *say* unto this mountain, be thou removed, and be thou cast into the sea; and shall *not doubt* in his heart, but *shall believe* that those things which he *saith* shall come to pass; he *shall have* whatsoever he *saith*: Therefore, I tell him whatsoever he *asks* for in prayer; *believe* and it will be his"

> *-the NIV Bible Mark 11:23-24*

Sounds simple, doesn't it? But how? How to toss out worrisome thoughts? It's not so simple. She repeats and repeats and repeats the scriptural words, over and over. In her mind, she sees that enlargement of her husband's lymph node washed into the ocean. She asks God for His peace because she *makes the choice* to believe, regardless of how she feels at this very moment of anxiety. No fear or doubt is allowed to linger. No fear or doubt is allowed to stay and make itself comfortable, to take up residence in her ponderings. She forces it to pass right on through as she thinks about these words of Christ. When He says "verily"; He means really, honestly, truly, absolutely, positively, a done deal, period, end of discussion! Negative, anxious thoughts are not from Him. No, not ever! She knows the source of the doubt: the evil one coming to try to steal her peace. This evil one wants her to doubt; wants her to take her mind off of His promises. She will not cooperate! She just will not allow it! No one can make her think what she doesn't want to think.

She experiences the peace of Christ in her soul as she continually reflects on His words, as she repeats them continually. Eventually, she feels the peace that goes way beyond her own understanding. She knows that He releases His awesome power through His word spoken, which reflects her faith in Him. She knows that as she repeats His healing promises, her faith in Him increases. It is not the speaking of these words, however important, as that is just the means to the end. It is the faith in Him that heals. His word tells her that the amount of faith needed is as very small as a mustard seed. She doesn't need to understand; just accept and believe Him, Continuously. His words aloud help her to grow in faith.

Ah ha, then the human factor enters: that all fall down and make silly mistakes. So the morning of biopsy day, her husband goes out to the routinely scheduled breakfast with his friends, and orders a glass of tomato juice. Now, this was after being told by the nurse, the hospital registrar, and his wife not to have anything by mouth for 6 hours prior to the biopsy except clear liquids. Drinking tomato juice causes the doctor to cancel the procedure. Clear means that one can see through it, like a window right? Hello! She thanks God for new mercies and grace everyday. So she goes onto a new day with the knowledge and faith that God is in control even when one screws up.

The biopsy is rescheduled for the following Tuesday at 9:30 in the morning. When she heard that it is to be conducted at The Cancer Center, her first startling thought was, "Are they really looking for cancer?" Her immediate answer is negative. She rationalized that it was only because that is where there is an operating room, machines, and staffing available on short notice. This is the explanation she offers herself.

But why, what is the big rush? Why does he even need short notice? This lymph node has been enlarged for the last 4 months and getting larger. She realizes then the problem. It's getting larger. Why is she even trying to figure it out? Her battle cry is: Two Cor. Ten Four! To her this means the scripture 2nd Corinthians, chapter 10, and verse 4. She *will* stand on the word of God; she *will* cast out fear and doubt. She *will* trust in her God, the Father. She *will not* allow the seeds of doubt and anxiety in her thoughts. It's up to her. She can control her thoughts.

The evening before this scheduled biopsy arrives; she prays. During the dark night she wakes with panic, "What if it's colon cancer and already spread to the lymph nodes? " She pleads with God that if her love was going to die to please take him quickly as she doesn't want him to suffer. She goes on to fret about where she might live. Sell this condo; it's too big for one person anyway? Sell the place at the lake and buy a smaller getaway to free up money? She was going round in circles in her mind! This seems to happen often in the darkness of night. She realizes that and wonders why. Then she remembers that Satan comes like a thief in the night to steal. But it goes on. Should she just liquidate everything and become a missionary in a third-world country? Yes, even that somewhat extreme option crossed her mind! She could not imagine everyday life without this man, lying next to her every night. Guilt was setting in, as well, because she knew the source of these thoughts. Just who did she trust? What happened to her resolve not to entertain such negative musings? "Stop it; just stop it!" she cries to herself. She knew God's will to be that everyone's body be healthy. Why was she losing sight of this? Not only did she know well the source of the negativity; but she was cooperating in, even entertaining, such ideas for a minute instead of forcing them out. She realized she was beginning to lose the battle. She immediately repented and went back to God's promises.

Start praising God! This strategy is the way out of the whirlwind of worry. Start praising. Praising is always her key to tamping down stress, anxiety, fear or the host of other emotions that can choke the breath out of her. Praise Him for His Word, for the sunshine, for hot fudge sundaes, for her family, for the freshness of spring. Praise Him for whatever she can think of that is worthy of praise. This works! Praise puts a big, bright, yellow and black octagon stop sign in her mind, in front of all those thoughts that aren't from Christ. After some moments in thankful prayer, peace eventually came and she slept.

Awaking in the morning on Tuesday, the big day; she appraises the whole middle-of-the-night frightening attack. When she thinks about the night before, she wonders how she managed to keep it together as further back; she had gone through two cancer diagnosis and many, many tests coming back positive with months of treatment during the past several years. Perhaps her memories of this time motivated her to pray for his quick death. But then again, perhaps that wasn't the cause. Only the mercy and grace given her through the word of God held her up and carried her through the treatment and the tests. Words spoken to her from her bible; and by her family and friends covered her. She reminds herself of this.

When the radiologist came in to see the patient for a few minutes to explain the procedure, he confirmed her worst worries. In response to her husband's question about "what exactly are you looking for?" The doctor answered simply "a malignancy". Okay so there it is, out on the table so to speak. As they wheeled him away, she told him she loved him and that Jesus loved him more. She prayed that he felt love and not fears on that long journey down the hall into the operating room. She felt only His peace surpassing any of her understanding; finally overcoming the horrid thoughts trying to set up camp in her mind.

She went out into the waiting area for a change of venue during the procedure. As she was reading and praying, praying and reading, a picture came to mind. The doctor would not be able to get anything when he put the needle in to extract the tissue to be analyzed. Further she saw the doctor, in her mind's eye, watching as the lymph node returns to its normal size. At first, she rejected this image, because during her prayers this past month, she thought the lymph node had been already returning to normal size. But as she went back to prayer; the same picture came back with even more vividness. So she said, "OK, Lord, then this is my prayer." Everything was going to be fine. How did she know for sure? The peace in her soul was the first indication. She felt this in her spirit. She thanked Christ.

She didn't really know for sure what this vision was all about: confirmation, hope, wishing, what? She did see it, however, as a gift from God. How did she know this? Because as she went back into the out patient surgery hall, about 25 minutes later; she practically collided with the radiologist who performed the procedure. He told her that when he first put the needle in, he could get nothing. Then he put it in again and drew out liquid. He watched the lymph node go down to normal size. "This is unofficial. You have nothing to worry about. I'm quite sure it was just a cyst. It is 'unofficial' as the sample still had to be sent out for analysis. You won't get the official results for 3-5 days," he told her. She was speechless. This is exactly what she had seen. This is exactly what God had shown her. What an amazing gift, an immediate answer to her prayers!

Overwhelmed with emotion, she could hardly speak. She uttered, "Hallelujah! Thank You God!" She felt nothing short of amazement that the thought and picture that came to her mind during prayer were actually occurring in the operating room. She repeatedly thanked her God, her Healer, her Comforter, and ever present Help in time of need. She couldn't stop thanking and extolling His faithfulness. As she called the children to report, she could hardly get the words out. "Everything's ok." She walked to the bedside and the nurse repeated what the doctor had told her, even the nurse was praising God!

She only hopes that if the news hadn't been good that she would have been praising and thanking Him anyway; because she knows that God would never leave or forsake her. Would she? Could she? It was time for her to thoughtfully examine this question. She decided the answer. When the official report comes in with questions about the cyst such as causes, possibility of recurrence, future possible prognosis or such; her resolve was to be that she would continue to thank God for her beloved's healing with more fervor as she waited.

She ponders, "Isn't trusting actually an action based upon one's beliefs? What does that word mean?" The word "trust" moves from her mind into her will, her action. She calls this truth to mind often as she fights the anxious fear continually trying to defeat her faith in Him, by sneaking into her thinking. Renewal of this truth had to occur often, as in everyday: every hour, or even sometimes, every five or ten minutes? She asks herself if she really believes. She ponders His Word, which is true.

> "Trust Me in your times of trouble, and I will rescue you, and you will give me glory."
>
> -the NLT Bible, Psalm 50:15

How He loves the little children who gather round His knee. They've done no wrong, except with no choice, were born of the lineage of the deceived Adam and Eve. Christ bids the little ones to come to Him. There is always a battle between good and evil going on for them. However, she knows the battle has already been won. She can be assured of this even as she watches the evil attack on young girls. The society, which values appearance over health, shows this behavior to be rampant. In a land of plenty girls sometimes just stop eating for fear of becoming overweight. Their bones, heart, and muscles are damaged for lack of nutrition. Other children suffer different issues as they become teens. The faith like that of a child often pulls them through various challenges. These three stories, similar to those handed down throughout history, shows hope, perseverance, and faith help all to grown in love for themselves, others and mostly for Christ, the Savior.

Satan Comes To Steal the Precious Children

The child's glowing face was sunken and sallow. The collar bones and knee bones protruded like steel pipes and knobs from her torso. Why was this beautiful child getting so thin? Doctors' exams and preliminary tests show everything to be ok. What was the cause? The family all go to God. Grandparents, aunts, uncles, cousins united in prayer with the distressed parents. Let this child of God, dear Lord, be well. Give the wisdom and peace of the Holy Spirit to all. All must agree to trust God; that He had heard their prayer; that He was doing a healing work as they spoke. They prayed in unity and love. This aggressive soccer player had to give up her beloved sport. She was a little tiger on the soccer field – small, quick, and ferociously determined to score goals or assists every game. And she always came through for the team. But now she was too weak to play. Please Lord, help her, and heal her. This youngest one heard a lie and took it into her heart. She knew no discretion yet. She didn't want to be "fat"; so she stopped eating and increased exercise to an unnatural degree. She was getting so very thin. She threw away her lunch at school, according to her sisters' accounts. One warm summer night, this child took a few licks of the vanilla ice cream cone, threw it away and started to jog around in the 90 degree weather. She didn't seem able to help herself. She couldn't handle the thought of the extra calories going into her body. Her face was dull. Her eyes seemed too big for the young face. Her internal organs are starving as well. She was taken to the emergency one evening with chest pains. Doctors' exams and preliminary tests show everything to be ok.

One night, after several months of praying to the Healer, and being coaxed to eat, a miracle occurred. The 10 year old was crying in her bedroom with Mom. They were discussing the direness of the need for her to eat. They were both weeping, out of concern and frustration; Dad overheard them. He went in and prayed with them. This young girl had committed her life to Christ previously. Dad told her the story of how even Peter, when fearful, denied knowing Jesus, not once but three times. He told her how in the Book of Acts 1:4 NLT Bible, Jesus told the apostles to wait: "Do not leave Jerusalem until the Father send you what he promised.. Remember, I have told you about this before. John baptized with water, but in just a few days you will be baptized with the Holy Spirit: Dad told his daughter then of how the apostles spoke more boldly Christ, of how they became stronger in Him. He asked her if she would like to ask God's Holy Spirit to heal her. "Oh yes" was the reply. All three prayed together. She felt hungry! She had a piece of buttered toast. She wanted chocolate cake. She had breakfast the next morning and has been eating fine ever since. Grandmother, of course, provided a chocolate cake the next day. Not obviously what a nutritionist would recommend. All were giddy with relief and thanksgiving. The goal was to gain 10 pounds in the next few months, before school started, so that soccer could once again become the choice for free time. This goal was achieved. It truly was a miracle healing – instantaneous! The bloom came back to her face, her energy returned. They heard again the sounds of her singing and laughing, so precious to all. Thank You Lord.

Soon after, another young cousin took on a similar gaunt appearance. Oh no, not her also? The girl complained when she ate about feeling sick. Her stomach hurt. At the choral concert, the thinness was so apparent. Comparing the bony legs, arms, face with those of the other fourth graders brought tears to the eyes of the mother and the grandmother. It was both tragic and scary to observers who knew her well. The child sang so beautifully, forming her mouth in a perfect "oh" as instructed by the music teacher. The marks in all of her academic classes continued to be high. Yet she was eating so very little every day. Energy drained away. Sitting on the sofa every afternoon, from after school until bedtime with no interest or ambition to even move; the child became so very quiet, withdrawn. Not only her body, but her personality was disappearing before everyone's eyes. The child's large brown eyes watched life passing her by; as she sat with no energy to participate. The doctors could find no answer. Gluten and dairy intolerance was perhaps the criminal stealing the life from her; yet tests didn't confirm. Continued visits to the doctors were frustrating with no definitive results. One even spoke of threatened in-patient care. The child's spark was gone, stolen. She was too exhausted and hungry to even smile or hardly speak.

Again, much united prayer was offered. Another miracle occurred. This young girl said to her Mom, "Maybe I would feel better if I just ate a little more." She started to eat, half sandwich by half sandwich. Prayers of thanksgiving increased when the pinkness on the child's face returned. She started introducing previously prohibited foods mouthful by mouthful, always with prayer shutting out her anxiety. Her body began looking normal and beautiful again. Energy and interest in things around her returned. Her beautiful smile returned.

Then another child princess of the King faces pain and surgery from an early age on. For the young cousin, who had trouble hearing since she was a toddler, a series of surgeries were scheduled throughout several years. As she grew into her pre-teen age, finally, the medical verdict is that nothing else can be done to help her hear better naturally. Somewhat sadly a hearing aid is ordered. With the strength of her God, this young teen drapes her beautiful blonde hair over her ear and proceeds in her life goals to honor her God. For now, this includes playing soccer, seeking straight A's in her high school curriculum, the expected developmental interest in boys as friends, working out and jogging, never stopping. She has learned a lesson beyond her years: that life sometimes offers challenges, small or large and that she can overcome whatever bounces her way; she bounces it back! This is a priceless lesson that takes many people much longer to learn. She is a trusting faith filled example to all of those around her.

> "Because you bend down and listen, I will never stop praying as long as I have breath."
>
> -the NLT Bible, Psalm 116:1

The grandmother, along with others, prayed in gratitude for these three young girls. She prayed in petition for all young girls subjected to the media always showcasing thin, beautiful, perfect bodies – at least beauty on the outside. Give them the wisdom and discretion to not believe all they see and hear. Keep them healthy. Let them make good, nutritional choices and lifestyles to build strong bodies. Help them to understand that they, each and every one, is a temple of the Holy Spirit. Let them guard and use their bodies in a holy way. Thank You Lord for your protection generated by your immense love of these children created in your image.

Some mornings, she awakes with a tinge of blue sadness touching her soul. No apparent cause comes to mind. She knows not why. Perhaps she is tired and needing rest? Is the need for a physical rest or the rest in Him? Anxiety tries to enter though she doesn't understand why her peace and joy leaves. She does know how to break the dangerous cycle before her. He has taught her in His word as she sits reading and quietly listening and thinking. She won't begin to think negative thoughts about what has happened, or why. She will focus on gratitude. Though sometimes very difficult to do, she must think only happy thoughts. She must visualize only happy times. She thinks back to better times. She sees pictures of fun times in her mind in her future. Her thinking is changing at her impetus of pondering more pleasant times.

Sun and Joy Return

The sun is back after several darker days. It mimics cycles of life. So bright to start; then crises occurs, often evolving into gloom. Questioning "why" occupies her thinking. Finally the tears of surrender wash away the darkness. Just as the rain washed the dark clouds from the sky; so it is with darker days of the soul. Worship to her Creator brings joy.

Bless each day that the Lord has made. Reaching for the rejoicing and being glad is not always an easy task. Finally after she mourns in the night, the joy comes in the morning. The sun breaks through the trees. It warms her heart as she surrenders to Him. The "why" of events is not important. Even the "what" of occurrences is of little concern? What matters is that she trusts. Trust *totally* in Him.

The beauty of creation all around is again evident. It softens the edge of grief. Questions remain unresolved; unanswerable. Joy seeps in slowly, but magically; however not by magic. The wand that touches to release the joy is this trust. This trust is born of recognizing the truly *unlimited love* of God for her. Incomprehensible Love that is so large and deep.

> "I prayed to the Lord, and He answered me; freeing me from all fears. Those who look to the Lord will be radiant with joy. "
>
> *-the NIV Bible, Psalm 34:4-5*

Sometimes she can't see the forest for the trees, so to speak. She gets bogged down in the details of her day. She lets her joy start slipping away.   She wants to learn to stop this before it develops within her an attitude of negativity.

Complaining

She starts to complain; whether it is about the daily cleaning tasks,-how mundane it is; or simply about what to make for dinner tonight. She dwells on all the irritating nit-picking details of her job repeated to her by her superior. "Why is that so important?" she mutters in her mind. Complaining can become a habit – assuredly and quickly. Instead she wants to be thanking her God that she has a place of her own to clean; and that she has the ability to do so. Thanking her God that she has choices about what to eat when and how to prepare it. She is glad that she has a job to go to everyday, with all of its niceties even if she doesn't feel like being nice at the moment. This is where she wants to be. She is always happy to welcome summer early. It is such a refreshing time to start another season. Why is she complaining? A slight sadness is felt.

This feeling of listlessness seems worse when she is tired or has too much on her day's agenda. She plans to kill each complaint immediately before the habit starts and grows. She knows that it grows and grows rapidly. It's like the dandelion on a hot sunny day, when she can almost watch it shoot higher and higher.

She takes a deep breath; exhales slowly; and looks all around to count her blessings. One by one by one, she counts. She even writes them. Oh, how many she can see when she really looks for them. She often takes them for granted, just because they are there. Just because the bright sun rises each morning, just because the coffee smells so exhilarating, just because the jelly slips off the buttered toast, she has so much. She acknowledges that much could be taken from her quickly; that horrible news can come swiftly. Her complaining turns from gray to blue to orange to bright yellow as it turns to complimenting her God for His blessings.

"The Lord is my Shepherd; I have everything I need. "

-the NLT Bible Psalm 23:1

She calls to mind that the phrase that is spoken the greatest number of times in her favorite book, her Bible, is "Do not be afraid. Do not fear." She remembers that He is always there and thanks Him for that knowledge and revelation that it is true. Happy is her heart; because of what she is thinking about.

PART II

Summer: The Beauty of Full Blossoming of Flowers and Relationships.

"A merry heart does good, like a medicine."

-the NIV Bible Proverbs 17:22

"Thank you for all the great laughter we've shared. You have a wonderful sense of always seeing the lighter side of life."

-Diana Booher

Summer

She can be free in summer,
To dance, to laugh, to walk at dark.
To hear the sounds of day
Merging into the night owl's cry,
To smell the blooms
More intense in the evening's coolness.
Oh summer, please don't go!

Fields of Gold

Fields of gold
Where once rain was,
Red poppies reaching and swaying
Brightness and gaiety so rich.
The smell of fresh cut grass,
Dandelions peeking through.
Peace flowing over like the blinding sunrise
Soon giving way to summer's burn.
There's hope now in the field of gold;
Where once rain was.
For tomorrows wished for,
Laughter and love.

She loves to get outdoors as spring turns into summer. Filling her unused muscles as well as her soul with freshness, she ambles down the path. She looks upward to the tall budding trees, farther still to the white billowing clouds constantly changing form. She breathes in deeply and exhales slowly restoring the radiance of reinvigoration. She skips across the little bridge, again reminding her that she is His child, that she is safe always and never needs to fear.

Walk in Early Summer

The rain has stopped. All smells so fresh and appears so shiny and glistening. Even the grass sparkles. She hears the woodpecker tapping out his evening song. The mocking bird sings his response. Tall wild grasses sway so gently in soft rhythm. No frogs are keeping time yet. Geese flutter as they leave the pond, startling her. A light twinkles on in a window. It paints warmth. Chill sets in as the sun is creeping down. Still a warm breeze caresses her; whisking away her cares. The early blooms send up sweetness to her being. Their fragrance and bits of color on a dull background just make her happy. Trees are yielding to the day's sun, now with blurred outlines. Muted leaves of different shapes throw shadows back and forth. A walk in spring brings renewal to her soul, refreshment to her spirit. Long awaited anticipation gives hope. She makes her way toward new beginnings, here, everywhere. New energy enters her. "What next?" she asks her God.

> "Create in her a new heart, oh God, And renew her with the right spirit. Fill her with your presence, Holy Spirit; That she may be taught, Comforted, encouraged and led.

Refocus her on the joy of your Salvation; for it refreshes her. Then she will be effective and Influential in helping others find you."

-the NIV Bible, Psalm 31:10

Quiet *can* bring His peace slowly. The coveted quietness causes His confident assurance to enter her spirit. She knows that she wants the stillness and its' resulting joy. Sometimes she can find it in beautiful music; as music opens her to the supernatural. But often, only utter silence will delight.

Quietness: Without, Within

It's quiet. All she hears are birds calling to each other. She wonders what they're saying. Are they questioning? Are they simply responding to a trill? Do they have a message, maybe even for her? Then, it's absolutely quiet for a few minutes. The birds have stopped singing. No sounds.

Is that the message? When she doesn't really know what all the chatter is about? Just be quiet? Be silent. Listen. She finds it difficult to be still; to stop the mind clutter whirling in her head. She finds it impossible to think of nothing. She has often wished for a switch to temporarily turn off her brain. The need to just be quiet is often and felt deeply. She wonders if maybe it's really a deeper need to slow down, rest and be alone. Something like the solitary wild daisy in the field, her thoughts seem to float whichever direction the breeze calls or leads or pushes. Is the daisy showing a kind of freedom? She thinks about being a young child, lying on the grass and watching as the clouds form beautiful castles in the sky. She knows she cannot truly go back to those uncluttered days; but she can touch that freedom again just by dwelling in their memories.

She ponders the clutter of the agenda ahead: a day of work, school, meetings and appointments. She's thankful that she is here, where it is peaceful for a few moments. Joyful peace comes easily and often to this placid place.

"Smile on your servant; teach her the right way to live."

-the NIV Bible Psalm 119:135

Silence

It's been said that silence is golden. It is precious. In a world so filled with a cacophony of noises, it is sought. Sometimes, the happy shouts and laughter of children playing send strains of music through the trees. A crescendo of joy fills all. Often, the contentment is heard in soft voices murmuring and glasses tinkling as friends catch up in a pleasant setting. Sometimes there is anxiety in the air as sirens shriek, a gun breaks the quiet with a quick cracking, hysteria screams, literally and fills the air as well. Sometimes the loneliness is deafening.

No matter which extreme or degree causing sweetness or pain, there comes at times the peace of silence. Not even the ticking of a clock is heard. The ambling of thoughts arise that result in problems solved, plans finalized creatively, motivation to do and then, finally wisdom. Silence is as essential to the human soul as air is to breathing life. No matter one's age, silence is a gift. This gift must be planned for, sought after, and then received and protected. It is to be kept and taken out from time to time as when fatigue overtakes the spirit. It is to be treasured. It is prayerful. This craving of the human soul must be satisfied; else one's bearings in life are lost. The way cannot be found until one stops and listens to the silence. It is often in the silence that she becomes closer to her God.

"Be still and know that I am...."

-the NIV Bible Psalm 46:10

Sometimes, she fears the unknown: food, places, people; all these and more. Unfamiliarity can bring positive anticipation; but often a cautious reluctance enters her. Strangeness brings uncertainty. Things look differently the second time around; but the first time can be disconcerting to her. She knows that the colors in her world change constantly, as she sees the same more and more, but looking different somehow. This is most true of the people in her life, even herself. She approaches life with the blindness of a child as newness comes to every event. Fear of the unknown only comes as result of various experiences that didn't turn out as expected. She has learned that getting to know people, who may seem upon first appearance "different"; can often bring unexpected rewards.

The Colors of People

Grandparents and grandchildren have mutually enlightening dialogue. She remembers when her young preschool granddaughter, during the dinner table conversation, asked her about color, "What color is cold? Is it gray or white or light blue? How about the color of an ice queen? What about the color of a hot pepper? Is it really red?" She mused about how to answer such questions.

Colors on the artist's canvas tell of the mood in the artist and in the picture captured. But a color of one's skin doesn't. She thinks about her neighbor. The two of them are so much alike, and yet so different, at least in outward appearances. Facial features shaped distinctively, skin of contrasting colors; but the sunny yellow shade of happy family memories shared by both of them. Each loves her children deeply. She knows that there is one true God who taught her about love; yet she realizes that she and the good friend each pray to different gods. Both have rich spiritual lives, each built on different foundations: one of rock and the other? Both have made their homes a safe sanctuary for their loved families. Each is filled with such contrasting mementoes of sacred memories. Each has different aromas of cultural food prepared to nourish those therein. They trade recipes. They support each other in problem solving about child rearing. They enjoy the same movies, and often listen to the same classical music. When listening to the blended sounds in a rhapsody or sonata, it isn't difficult to see varying colors and hues in the sound waves. This is true in people, different, but oh so similar.

They have different favorites; just as they have experienced different childhoods. They help each other in time of need as good neighbors do; showing and sharing love. There is peace in this little community, bound by geography.

Lessons to be learned, as certain degrees of familiarity do not breed contempt, as sometimes warned. Rather perhaps an understanding of diverse roads taken is born. Hers is a familiar path, guided by close family. Her friend's is one less taken – leaving her parents and homeland in another country, even another continent.

Yet as they come to know and understand each other; they come to love each other. Accepting different cultural habits, foods, even language becomes so easy when individuals are seen as individuals, not applying gross ethnic generalities. These are incidentals that don't diminish the truth of all being made in the image of the great Creator. Did they come to understand each other simply because they are neighbors? Not so much; but really because they spend time together. Sometimes it is a quick hello, or a favor asked and returned, or a relaxing cup of tea together. Time well spent as each becomes more and more familiar with ways different from her own; for this kind of familiarity leads to understanding. The lesson to appreciate, even celebrate the differences while understanding that each just wants to love and be loved. For that is why each is made.

> "The growth of understanding follows an ascending spiral; rather than a straight line. You show me your world; and I will show you mine"

-Joanna Field, <u>Girlfriends</u>

She sees and feels the joy in their hearts; that which has not yet been tarnished by the difficulties and the tragedies of life. She learns from them to adopt their freeness daily. She wants them to know that she is here on a mission from God to help them grow; to keep their joy through all that life has planned. She realizes that they are teaching her how to enjoy thinking and acting young again; how to be open to newness and freshness. Such fun! She vows to never lose this lesson. The faith of a child is beautiful to behold, and to imitate.

Communicating with Grandchildren

Her children thought she always asked too many question, especially during their teen years. The difference between interest and interference is small and wide at the same time. The responsibility of parenting seemed ever so huge to her. But now, the grandmother's role today takes on different dimensions. The challenge to communicate with this new generation occupies her. She has much to offer the precious sons and daughters of her sons and daughter. As she ages, how much more valuable life becomes to her. So many lessons have been learned. So much wisdom has been sought and received. The love she feels for them is so profound. She is more aware of the pitfalls into which they could slip and fall; than she was with her own children. She was too busy to think about it. The perspective of a grandparent is almost indefinable. She knows that she, most likely, will leave this life before them. Yes, they will have their parents for a long, long time but parents don't have the same viewpoint. They can't. It is directly opposed to the responsibility they meet. The perspective that comes as a result of long experience in living is different somehow. What meaningful reminder can she leave, beyond the priceless memories made? How to tell them? They are growing into adults. They are teetering on the brink of independence. This season of her life offers a special opportunity as the landscape has changed. In this day of technology, shortened words, not spoken face to face but often screen to screen, how to talk now is much more challenging. Where would she be without emails, texting, and other electronic wonders to keep in touch? To not intrude on the busy lives; but to keep aware of events and issues they may be experiencing. An opportunity given to initiate or respond whenever so moved. Is there another more lasting way to stay connected after she's gone? Face to face communication is definitely the best way; but not always possible.

She looks for ways to speak to these loved beings as they may be scattered across the city or the country, even across the oceans. Not so often anymore are they found down the block, or just across the street. She cannot always put her arms around her grandchildren to hug or comfort.

But she can encircle them with prayer and the word of God. She can help them to see and to be the glory of God here on earth! She can assist them to grow in that glory as they mature and face all of the challenges that life will hand them: reacting as Jesus would; if and when they are open to such suggestions. How many ever experience talking to Christ face to face; like Abraham? Now most rely on the Book, maybe an electronic book, but still a book. The written word is the primary way, second to prayer to bring light to one's thinking. As grandparents' questions are continued, God's answers are sought. She wants them to hear her reinforce His words after she is gone. When they face trials, to be hopeful and radiantly successful; she gives them one more reminder to trust Him.

Grandparents have the unique chance to help cement sound values and lifestyles, taught by their parents. Even these if not taught by the parents. Grandparents are generally not overwhelmed with working so hard to put food on the table, driving them to school, sports events, dentist appointments, shopping for school supplies, chauffeuring to and from birthday parties, teaching them to drive, ad infinitum. What a truly golden season of opportunity it is before the grandparents; should they decide to take it.

She thinks back to the baby and toddler years and beyond. She spends time pouring over old photos. She writes each a letter to keep wherever life may find them residing. She reminds them of their special personality tendencies, evident to her when watching them play, even as young three and four year olds. She writes of the special gifts each have been given. She confirms the unconditional love given by the parents and self. She encourages them continually in the letter, even after she is not here physically. She hopes that they will treasure what she believes to be wisdom and keep the writing safe. She sees them in her mind, opening it and rereading from time to time, as they mature in the roads they choose to follow. She asks them to reserve a spot on their bookshelves during the coming years, to keep it nearby. She wants them to take it out and read it whenever they feel the need; no matter their age or where they live.

She remembers her own mother, speaking of a letter she once wrote to her children. She knows not where that letter is. She never had an opportunity to read it. She sometimes runs across her Mom's signature inside an old book. Sometimes this is enough to give her a moment of comfort; it has to be for now. But how she wishes she had that letter or such a letter to read and reread.

In this later season, grandparents have a moment to take a breath. They take this gift of time to help the following generation, in so very many different ways, grow into the radiance of following God's will, of trusting Him to answer their prayers.

This is true not only for biological grandparents; for many have the role of spiritual grandparents. They are praying and conjuring up thoughts of sons and daughters of foster children, adopted children, or even children well-mentored in which a physical, mental, emotional, or spiritual need was met.

> She asks God to "give them a complete understanding of what He wants to do in their lives, and she asks Him to make them wise with spiritual wisdom. Then the way they live will always honor and please the Lord and they will continually do good kind things for others. All the while they will learn to know Him better."

> *-the NLT Bible, Colossians 1:9-10*

This is her prayer, not only for them but even for herself, as well. Never finished with the privilege of His work, she looks for ways to heal the sick, to cast out demons, to spread His love. She prays, even now, for all.

She truly values all of her friends, old ones of many years, and new ones with whom a spark of connection starts and grows to a blaze of love. This is her story of a friendship held for many years, starting when she was preschool age.

A Friend of Many Years

She's had a friend since childhood. She lived just around the corner from her when they were young, starting their lives together as toddlers. They listened to their mothers visiting. They remained friends now after living so many different experiences.

Old enough to start school, this priceless tall friend coaxed the shy, little one to kindergarten. The weapon of coercion was a box of cheese flavored crackers as the tall one chanted, "A few more steps, and I'll give you two more crackers". The shy one was crying, not wanting to go to this strange place called "school" without her Mom. She would take a couple of steps and hold out her hand for another two cheese crackers. Then she would take one step closer. A couple of bites seem to strengthen her courage to face the unknown. It most likely was the concern and love with which they were offered. This is characteristic of the tall one. This friend has walked beside her or even a little ahead of the shy one, often through the years. Elementary through high school through marriages and babies, losing contact for a few years and then picking back up; the connection continues. They don't meet often now, living on different sides of the state. She wishes this wasn't so. She wishes that by walking around the corner, she could go and knock on the door, have a cup of tea, sit and talk and laugh and talk and laugh; and solve all the problems of their worlds. Even now, when they do connect in a nearby city or by phone or electronically, this sense of love is still there. They can talk openly about anything. They trust each other. The long history they share can never be replicated or replaced. When she thinks of her friend, she sends a prayerful smile up in her thoughts for this treasure.

A special quality of this friend is that she laughs often and freely, at peace with herself-the wisdom of many years' living sparkles through. Another priceless quality is that ambition is still strong in this treasured friend: finishing a college degree when turning 60 years old; on an academic scholarship no less! She shines for others every day. Constantly interested in sisters and brothers and children and grandchildren of each other, they update when they talk. A widow too early; gracious survival and the way to find joy were modeled by the tall one. No complaints about what life has handed or taken away are ever heard. The tall one just has fun appreciating and making the most of each day. This wise woman views each day as a gift to be opened and enjoyed.

Memories from many years ago another gift! Going to elementary and high school together; they saw each other daily. A bond was formed walking to and from school; it is so deep that it cannot be broken. Getting into trouble together more than a few times; often for giggling uncontrollably during ninth grade English offered spice in their growing years.

One particular occasion; with mischievous scheming, when the shy one landed a part in the senior play and the tall one didn't. They stole into school very early the next morning. Together, these "partners-in-crime" put pieces of stinky limburger cheese up on the high light fixtures in their classroom and left with the heat of the lights turned on. They had to stand on the desks to reach the old ice-cube-tray-like light fixtures. They left quietly and quickly, unnoticed. When the school day started, the entire second floor smelled horrific! To their knowledge, the "powers that be "never found out. Or maybe it was just decided to ignore it and chalk it up to "senioritis"?

Often in their later teen years, if one of them could talk their parents into lending them the car; they would go a few hours away to the beach. Was it because they loved the water? Not necessarily; but rather because that's where the boys were. They enjoyed a freedom that their own children couldn't. The world seemed safer in days gone by.

She recently received a photo of the two of them: the shy one and the tall one, in the mail, taken in the second grade. It's precious! It brings back so many memories that make her smile. She appreciates this bond so much.

As this tall friend traveled across the state to celebrate the 50th wedding anniversary of the shy one, her humor showed in the box of Cheez-Its given as the gift!

Still very physically attractive; still possessing that beautiful skin and smile that the shy one envied her for in their teen years. Of course also, sharing her beautiful heart and spirit made even more so with the passing life experiences.

As both of them are now in the last third of their lives, this bond is valued even more highly. This kind of a friend is an experience in loving relationships that comes not often. It's irreplaceable.

> "Friendship is unnecessary, like philosophy, like art it
> has no survival value; rather it is one of those things that
> give value to survival."
>
> -C.S. Lewis

She has learned that it is fun to be a "kid'; in conversation, in some activities, in attitude. She knows there are times when she must put away the things of childhood. Yet she hangs onto the memories with glee because she has also learned that she will forever be young in the eyes of the Lord. She can always depend on Him, trust her troubles to Him, and continue to walk in enjoyment and laughter because He will always be with her. He doesn't want her to be walking heavy-laden. She cannot spread His kingdom of love in the many small ways possible if she is troubled. She works continually to think about this truth as troubles in her world try to distract her. Just as a couple of Cheeze-Its offered her strength, so His word offers her strength to take the next few steps.

> "My friends are my estate. Forgive me then the avarice to hoard them!"
>
> *-Emily Dickinson*

It's been said with lightness by comedian, Erma Bombeck, that a friend doesn't go on a diet because you are fat; or doesn't defend a husband who gives his wife an electric skillet for her birthday. True? As she and her friend notice, every year, more signs of aging in their bodies; they decide to fight the good fight…of aging together.

What Price Vanity?

Ah yes, the fight against aging, the fight that never stops! Why can't one keep the same wrinkle-free skin and neck? Why can't one keep the slim midriff? Why can't one keep the smooth hands? Why can't one avoid gray, white, and all shades in between on her head? Well, theoretically she can control this unwelcome sign-simple as coloring her hair. Actually in the summer, this supposed "crown of glory" is worse. The bright sun bleaches all color out and dries out the once silky mane. Often, something very close to white appears at the temples and the cowlick in the back of her head. Most unflattering and most aging! She and her friend decide to fight this fight of "old" hair together. They definitely do not subscribe to the group that claims to have earned every gray hair and therefore won't touch it. Well, have at it. It's just not for her.

To the hair color counter with so many shades and choices is the next step. The box that promises to beautify with the sun-kissed look is just what she wants. Sounds great! Note that it promises "sun-kissed", not dry and straw-like as is how her hair could be described presently.

The first step is to put on the one-size-fits-all tissue thin plastic gloves. Then open bottle #1. Of course unscrewing the tight top of bottle #1 in these gloves that are way too large is almost impossible!

Where is her best friend to help? The next challenge is presented: pour bottle #2 together with #1. Then, before mixing, break the tip off of the larger bottle so that air can presumably escape and the chemicals don't explode in one's hands or face. Shake until totally mixed. Another challenge faced with slippery, large gloves; don't let a drop escape on the pretty rug beneath her feet. Now, section the hair to show all the graying white roots. Ugly! Very ugly! Squirt this darkness onto one's scalp. Isn't there a warning somewhere in the beauty or health magazines about these chemicals causing cancer? Within minutes the creamy liquid turns even darker.

Applying to all the roots should be easy as the bottle has a small spout to ensure getting the dye where one wants it, and only where one wants it. Mmmmm...don't think so! Where is her friend to help? The collar of her pink and white striped terry robe is now turning dark gray to dark brown to black. Wonder if that is happening to the hair strands as well. Uh-oh, a couple drops runs down to the floor. Make a note that in the future to wear her oldest t-shirt and to remove all rugs or to cover all carpet underfoot with a painter's drop cloth! Where, oh where is her friend to help! The timer is set for 15 minutes plus 5 to cover "stubborn gray". Although she is instructed to keep the gloves, now slimy and black, on until the timer rings, what in the world can be done for 20 minutes with hands covered with this goop? While waiting for her friend and for the required minutes to pass, she busies herself in the kitchen. This is where the surfaces are hard and can immediately be cleaned of the dark yuck that seems to be melting, now when a drop or two unexpectedly hit the countertop. This is the only option. She definitely doesn't want anything else, besides the terry cloth robe to be permanently dyed this horrid shade of shiny gray-black. Of course she needs to constantly also wipe this now runny stuff off her forehead and her neck as it certainly does a great job of dying one's forehead and neck. Hope it takes as well on the grayish whitish hair. She's trying to make a cup of coffee to enjoy with her friend upon the expected arrival.

Maybe in the winter with much sun lacking, one could try to dye one's face with a summery light golden blonde – quicker and more convenient and less expensive than a tanning booth, right? Although this certainly wouldn't be recommended by the producer of the hair color!

She was also instructed in the directions, to comb her hair into the "preferred hair style". What? There are two assumptions here. One: that she has a hair style. Two: that it is the preferred style. Obviously the person who wrote these "simple" instructions did not have fine, curly hair and live in a humid climate! There are a few charming ringlets, as they are often referred to in romantic novels; but generally her hair looks like it was caught in a fan turned on high. If her friend was here, perhaps she could find a desirable hair style for her. One that was glamorous, youthful, and carefree. Or at least one she could prefer!

Time of waiting is over. Wash the runny dark liquid out now with warm water. Apply the wonderful conditioner that came in the box with the product. Done with great expectations! She pats her head to remove any excess water, applies another product to the roots to give this flyaway stuff some body and turns on the hair dryer; waiting to see shiny, sun kissed smooth, beautiful, magnificent, young-looking hair. She wishes her friend would hurry and come and dry her hair for her. By now, she is too tired to turn her head upside down as she dries, to "maximize fullness"; so she just blows it dry standing in front of the mirror.

Turning off the dryer, and taking a good look; she realizes that it is not sun kissed, it is strawberry kissed. She never really had red hair, or even wanted it but now her head definitely has a reddish halo, except, of course, where the reluctant white hair didn't take the color. So decision time is here. What price vanity? Go to a salon and pay much more for a good color treatment or just go natural? Natural means gray, or white, streaked unattractively with the straw-like blonde. No way, will try again with a different shade! Refuse right now to have "aging" hair – too young! That's how she feels.

Coffee's ready. Doorbell rings. In walks her friend with the most beautiful sun-kissed shade of hair. And the style is so now and up-to-date, magnificent and young-looking. Really? Really!

Should she accidently spill her friend's coffee on her? No! Never! She won't ever do such a thing, even though she may have thought it. Perhaps it's better just to smile and compliment her, not reminding her about their date to color their hair *together*? The new look and color do take a few years off! What price friendship?

> "It is one of the blessings of old friends that you can afford to be stupid with them."
>
> *-Ralph Waldo Emerson*

She loves being "silly" with her family and friends. A smile, a laugh from deep within makes life easier sometimes even tolerable. Let her not to forget to think like a child about all disappointments, large or small. Let her not forget to brush them off and fix these problems later, like the color of her hair. Let her run and skip with the abandonment of a child, with her tresses flying behind her.

Old houses speak to her of memories and happenings long ago. Her childhood home tells her of fun and voices and parties and conversation. The baby grand piano in the living room, under which she and her younger sister would hide to watch TV until they giggle aloud and the older sister heard them. They would take off in a wild slippery run in pajamas and slippers, escaping the older sister, laughing all the way up the stairs. She remembers the old white kitchen table and the fruitwood dining room table, different sizes, different colors for different meals and gatherings. She remembers the wooden, army style, bunk beds in which her brothers slept. Her mom's scalloped-edged end table arranged with figurines. Yet she doesn't feel compelled to furnish her home with what are now antiques even though she values the old.

Hidden Value

That style of "shabby chic": a mixture of contemporary, traditional, cottage and painted furniture has captivated her eye and her heart for her home. She loves the triumph when she finds that special treasure, that brings back some of those memories that warm her heart. Her shopping friends all complimented her confirming her choice. It is the thrill of the hunt which goes way back to her ancestors. Only now she hunts and forages, not for fowl and fish and berries. Now she hunts in resale shops. She searches for items to make her nest more comfortable and complete. Furniture to look at and ponder about; painted furniture she believes to be the best! Unique dressers or cabinets; with unusual little drawers or shelves in which to stow special precious treasures are the best. Some look in great shape with beautiful distressing, over the original color. Some don't function well with drawers that stick or doors that won't stay latched. Some have ugly chips out of the surface. But each one is priceless even though the there is no rhyme or reason for the amount printed on the sales ticket. Each piece has its' spirit of the past covered; repurposed for a new and different use.

Is this how all her friends and she are, with souls, as well as bodies, all shapes, sizes, and conditions? Some repainted, smooth, shiny, and protected; some are rustic with scars, dents and scratches visible. Yet all are priceless and waiting to love and be loved. Valued differently often, by a society with a somewhat, superficial measuring stick. Has beauty and value always been only in the eye of the beholder?

In the eyes of the Creator, each and every one, is worthy of His immeasurable love. Is each and every one, capable of returning it; reluctant to submit totally and thus missing the plan, the peace, the divinely designed purpose? Does each even know about it? Only in recognizing and using one's special gifts, one's unique design can true joy in doing be found. She skips through the day with special plans just for fun.

> "Come Saturday morning, I'm going away with my friend. We'll travel for miles with our Saturday smiles Just me and my friend, will Saturday spend 'til the end of the day. And then we'll move on, but we will remember, long after Saturday's gone."

> *-music by Fred Karlin,*
> *Lyrics by Dory Previn*

Sometimes the chill of the rainy day creeps into her home, into her bones, even into her heart. It is the advent of distressing news of her grown child's happiness being threatened. He brings devastating news, news that he must bring to his parents; of his wife leaving.

Divorce

It's an almost frosty Sunday when the son comes to visit. He talks to them. He tells of the circle of family, breaking. The parents are dismayed. "How could it be this bad? Why? What happened? What went wrong?"

"No, there is no hope," is his reply. The dampness settles in as they think about such coldness seeping into the home in which their grandchildren will be raised. This coldness that will seep into the children's hearts as well.

Was it true love in the beginning? That just didn't grow with the years, with the children born of this union? Or was it an instantaneous decision, without much thought or prayer? Or perhaps one person was more in love than the other? Was the commitment not equally shared? Was either or both not up to the responsibility of home and family? An impulse action, without thinking, that could not be forgiven? A career that took inappropriate, life threatening precedence over people and relationships needing nurturing, may have been the impetus for this tragic split? Why? How could it have gotten so far?

The children are subverted by the shock. They stand in the middle of the storm. Waiting, waiting to see which way the wind of change will blow. Will they be swept into the nothingness of confusion and loss? Living in two homes at the same time, as forgetting their math and composition books because of leaving it in the other bedroom, in the other house is difficult to explain. Their classmates listen to the faltering explanation given to the teachers. Two separate birthday celebrations are not really twice the fun. Family meals with one stark, empty chair. Always wishing for the circle to mend, the children cry softly in the dark. They hope. They scheme. They plan. They sob. They act out their sadness and their anger. They love both parents deeply. They blame themselves. Guilt tries to destroy them. They vow to never become parents themselves because they won't even risk breaking the hearts of their children.

Does it have to be? The pain rips them. Will they scar forever? Will they mend? Such grief they have not known in their young lives. Anxiety takes over. What is the answer? The only way to mend a broken heart, to recover from any tremendous loss is prayer. She knows this. She provides support when and how, in many different ways, in any way she can to these lost souls. She trusts that the love of God will make and keep them whole and steady them through the rough waters ahead. Striving, praying, and believing, that the children will find themselves out of the troubled state. Who knows what scars will remain, unsettled, hidden? She can only go in prayer, to the Father for rest.

> "I took my troubles to the Lord. I cried out to Him, and He answered my prayer."

> *-the NLT Bible Psalm 120:1*

She was watching him, this man she admired from afar. He was being interviewed on a television show. She had read his book about overcoming cancer; about the way he was using his millionaire winnings to help children fight their battle with this disease. She felt dismayed, let down, that after all he was only human, making poor choices and suffering the results. She hopes for him to find his way.

The Athlete Disgraced

The humbled athlete speaks of his fall. He is sorry now. His eyes, his pride, his winning spirit blinded him from truth. He lost his titles, so important to him, his identity. He loves his children. He wanted not to leave a legacy of deceit to them. He weeps. He knows he cannot change the past. Unwittingly, he is asking for mercy. Unknowingly, he is seeking the Author of forgiveness. She prays for him. Holy Spirit, open his mind and heart to the Truth. Failure after failure has worn him down just as win after win had taken him higher.

He wants to compete again in his beloved sport. Wisdom eludes him right now. Confusion reigns. He is walking a rocky road, trying not to slip and fall again. He speaks of a process taking place. He is patient. All the good with his earnings and effort, he had accomplished through his battle with and for cancer victims has become tarnished. Underneath the dullness lies still the brightness of gold. He knows not where the road sign is to lead him from the dimness on the path before him; to reach the brightness, to have the sheen return.

His deep love for his children will help to guide him. He will find purpose again. Love will light the way. The light is in the face of Jesus. The children's love reflects this. Does he realize this yet?

Each makes mistakes, sometimes very large ones that become public. Sometimes such that strip one's God-given dignity. Or at least that is what is felt. She asks forgiveness for her own stupidity at times hurting others. She realizes that each is only a human being; flawed but capable to receive His great love and grace, His inconceivably unlimited forgiveness and mercy. She begs this for all. It is freely given and received by faith.

> "We are all merely moving shadows and all our busy rushing ends in nothing."

> *-the NLT Bible Psalm 39:6*

They moved into what she fondly calls their "retirement cottage". Lots of windows overlooking beautiful tall trees; yet it's just a few short blocks from her church, her friends, the mall. A place she was always attracted to want to live there – beautiful black topped, curving roads lined with fields of bright flowers. It is a cozy place that makes her smile every day.

Window Coverings

The new home brings gratefulness. Making a decision about window coverings for all these windows can confuse. A small space with many, big, beautiful windows looking out on pine trees, it is a haven, a sanctuary. The colorful birds and the flitting butterflies catch one's eye continuously on a summer afternoon. Why have any window coverings, she wonders. Are they really needed? Privacy is not an issue. The sunshine is pouring in is wondrous sensation of warmth and light. Will it be too much in the heat of July? This home has a soft peaceful feeling, almost a holy place. Will this aura be enhanced or compromised if the windows are covered?

Cost estimates bring sticker shock, not hundreds but thousands of dollars. Reluctantly, realization gives into the knowledge that it must be done: to protect. To protect from what she ponders: the fading of the sun, the eye of an intruder, the shock of lightning storms? All based on "ifs." How easy it is to become bogged down in her thinking.

Are these shades like those of her heart? Why? Why is this done? Where does the fear come from? Of what is she afraid? Embarrassment, false pride, regret of past days? The lowering of the shades of one's soul brings partial darkness. God knows all of her innermost secrets. She is not really unique. She is loved. She is safe. These coverings are but a shield against the winds of turmoil that can rock; against the hurts that can pain. She learns to open the barriers until it is a sheer film of golden hope. The eyes of her heart and soul are lifted to see refreshment. This temple is flooded with hope for the future peace and brightness, as openness, clarity and honesty are experienced.

She thinks about the sincere openness she can share with a true friend, not afraid to be honest and direct. Knowing that she can trust a confidence spoken to only the friend, she bares her heart and soul, just as she would like to leave her windows bare. For then the sense of burden is lifted and instead transparency arrives, a pleasant, relaxed, peaceful exchange of thoughts and ideas. No cloudiness, only clarity is seen, is heard in the words spoken. Heaviness of heart is ended. Thanksgiving is uttered. She decides on shades that melt into the woodwork when open. She leaves them open all the time. Yet they are there, when or if needed.

"Send forth your light and your truth; let them guide me."

the NIV Bible, Psalm 43

She thanks her God for the relationships that He has brought into her life. She prays for them often, asking God to bless them. She asks how she can be the kind of friend to show His love always. She realizes that is what being a friend means.

What Is A Friend?

She thinks about what a friend is...a confidant, companion, crony, buddy, classmate, roommate, ally, co-worker, peer, associate, team mate, sister, brother, mother, dad. Is a friend all of these and more; and even sometimes less?

A good friend, the kind that doesn't come along every day, is an encourager, that is someone who really listens when she talks to them. It is one who takes her side when the world seems to be against her. When she wants an opinion on her hair, make-up or a new outfit; one is willing to answer her honestly. Sometimes even when she doesn't want an honest opinion, she gets one! When facing a problem an honest discussion with a trusted cohort wanting only what is good for her always can be valuable. A friend will graciously share her chocolate. Even when overwhelmed and can't pray, a prayer warrior, interceding for her, stands ready. If incapacitated, help arrives by one who is willing to lend a hand; sometimes even walking in with mocha. She receives calls or texts from loved ones just to check in with her. She feels appreciated and loved by those around her who accept her unconditionally. "Yeah, but so what; why worry? It's really no big deal!" is the response she hears when she needs it. Large and small celebrations are shared. As she thinks about just what a friend is; she wonders if she can really be a friend, live up to such expectations. Can she? Is she? She thinks about who this sounds like. Who possesses all of these qualities, and many, many more to an unlimited degree? Can she imitate this Friend? Does she strive to do so?

> "Greater love has no one than this that he lay down his life for his friends…I have called you friend."

> *-The Bible, John 15:13, 15*

Only the development of friendships with Jesus, her family and others have value forever. Nothing else in this earthly life matters.

> "We are involved in a life that passes understanding and our highest business is our daily life."

> *-John Cage from*
> *"Where Are We Going and What Are We Doing?"*

Part III

Autumn: The Glorious Colors of Her Country.

The Artist

The flaming leaves,
Unmatched,
In their boisterous proclamation:
"Autumn is here!"
Bright crimson,
Orange and gold,
Yellow, darkness like black green,
Fading to lemony crème

.

Oh, so beautiful the painting!
Who is the Artist?

"And so while others miserably pledge themselves to the pursuit of ambition and brief power I will be stretched out in the shade, singing."

-Fray de Leon

"He who smiles rather than rages is always the stronger."

-Japanese wisdom

"If my people who are called by my name, will humble themselves and pray and seek my face and turn from their wicked ways, then I will hear from heaven and forgive their sin and will heal their land."

-the NIV Bible, 2 Chronicles 7:1

She thinks, as the autumn of her years approach, about much. She ponders life's journey: where she's been, where she is, where she's going. Choices made and choices to be made, roads traveled good and bad, always learning. Not finished yet, not really ready to stretch out in the shade and spend her remaining time singing as Fray de Leon (preceding page), she ponders…

One's Life: One's Destiny

She realizes now that daily decisions actually do become one's destiny. Daily decisions determine how she is spending the life, the time given her. These decisions are directly linked to her thought life. As her thoughts bring emotions, then motivation to act, she now understands somewhat how her thoughts become her life. The few big choices that she made don't have the greatest impact on how her life was spent so far. That is, choices such as, where she lived, the career she choose, even whom she married; while important didn't influence her destiny as much as the smaller ones, made every day. Such large seemingly-defining choices do nothing more than present an ever-changing set of circumstances. These circumstances may be good or bad, easier or more difficult, fun or troublesome trials. Where she lives, with whom, and what she does to gain sustenance does not determine the substance of her life. These preferences may influence the amount of hard work she is choosing as the circumstances are sometimes more difficult with which to cope without an equal partner, or enough money for essentials, or a less than favorable reaction to life's inevitable stressors. But what *really* sets her course? Maps her journey?

Rather, strength or weakness results; as she wanders down the path of life. Being lost or not depends on the light shining on this path. What or who guides? The true Light and Way is available to all, any day, everyday, anytime, all the time. The ins and outs, the little alternatives picked each day seemed so insignificant, unimportant. Oh, but these did and continue to determine her destiny. She chose to search for and find the true Light. For it is the true Light shining down, showing where and how to step that guides to joy. Is time well spent or wasted? Are relationships built or destroyed with words spoken? What words? Are reactions spurred by love or anger? Is the day an act of worship or is it a day of complaining and negativity? Is there a purpose in the daily decisions or are they random? Are reactions controlled without thought and by whim? Are goals clear or muddled, unsure? Only walking in the true Light assures enough brightness on the road to lead her to peace and joy, the desired destiny. Only truly walking with God assures that shadows cast by mountains on her path don't cause devastating falls into deeply unreachable pits. Only truly living in Him and He in her, will be the fortress, the shield to protect through difficulties and trials. Only this habit of thought will deflect the shooting arrows of life aimed at her. Such arrows may maim but will not destroy. Her attitudes, beliefs, reactions, and choices become enlightened by Him as she walks the well-lit path. She is able to straighten, when stumbling on a rock thrown down. Only with and through Him, will she find her joyful destiny, as presented by Mark Batterson, in his book <u>Draw the Circle</u>. Many of these thoughts came to her as she read Batterson's books. Many came to her as she thought and prayed about it.

She considers the elected leaders of her country and how their decisions affect her. It's a huge job running a country, state, or city. It isn't her job, she realizes with great relief. Her job is to vote the qualified candidate and pray for her government. She knows there is only one kingdom that is operated without fault or mistakes; and that it is not of this world. Meanwhile she prays with the faith of a child for her governors to be filled with the wisdom of God.

"You can tell what they are by what they do."

-interpreted from the NIV Bible by the author, Matthew 7:16

Every night, she reviews the day and often, plans the next as though the next is a given. She feels so blessed to be able to have many choices, sometimes too many. She must decide. She asks His help in planning her day.

Work of Today

Her agenda is full. How much of it is important? How many minutes and hours are used up on things of temporal value? The house to be straightened, the leaves to be raked, the food to be prepared into loving meals, the cookies to be baked, the laundry to be washed and put away, the internet communicating to be accomplished, the TV. Stolen moments will never to be given again. Of what value is it all?

You are not calling her to lead a monastic life. This she knows. You are calling her to enjoy all of the blessings you have to give, here and eternally. You are calling her to share the Source of her abundance of spirit. How can this full agenda of work, granted that much of it pleasant, from which she truly reaps satisfaction, be your will for her? It seems that it is of such temporal value. Or is it? Does it have any significance for eternity? What is important to you today, Lord of all? How can this full agenda with a long, ever-increasing "to do" list be narrowed down? Does how she is spending this equally-given resource, 24 hours today, please you? Where, how should she build your house, Lord, instead of being concerned with hers? How can she? Build it to be used by you today for those less fortunate caught in the storms of life? Build it today to be used for loving relationships? Guide her priorities that her order for today becomes yours; that her effort and activity be spent today be used to spread the good news of you and your redeeming love. Help her to enjoy tremendously the blessings, the gifts and the earnings.

Her goal becomes her prayer. Her prayer takes concrete shape as her day unfolds. Work is worship to our God. It all makes sense to her now. Let her use today as though it is her last: loving others and showing His love no matter what the day brings. What makes the difference each day? What gives her work today eternal value? What gets her out of her "thinking" chair each day, with a smile on her face, to meet the day? It is her attitude and answer to why she is using her time in this specific way. How privileged she is to walk in this beautiful state of knowing Him. Even the days of doing the nitty-gritty chores of seemingly insignificant value can have purpose. Well, not too sure about cleaning the bathroom; but "someone's gotta do it"! Even the difficult tasks become a prayer as His wisdom guides her. Immersed in grace, days become only cause and opportunity for joy and thanksgiving. Peace rains down upon her. She knows that He parts the sea of each and every crisis for her to cross to goodness. Even, at times, carries her across the water and sets her in the promised land. For this is a land she loves; where she can sing and dance in praise. She thanks Him for her work. Let it always glorify. She thanks Him for these special God-designed, not chance, opportunities to share His love with others.

> "In fact, the best prayer doesn't even involve words at all; the best prayer is a life well lived. All of life is meant to be a prayer, just as all of life is meant to be an act of worship."

> *-The Circle Maker by Mark Batterson, p.140*

*A **disturbed*** young man shoots his way into an elementary school. He randomly opens fire, killing young ones and staff alike. The newscasters bring continuing details as the media is focused exclusively on this horrific act. Interviewing mental health professionals and legal professionals as well, an answer is sought. Is he venting some horrible anger or has an evil spirit taken over, totally controlling him? Couldn't he have been stopped? Watching as the news unfolds across this land becomes even more saddening as...

Her Nation Mourns

The moms and dads cry in anguish. How can this be? The little ones were shot...and killed...at school? It makes no sense. It isn't right! It is so difficult to accept; almost impossible as deep, wrenching sadness fills all, wondering how to face another morning. God help them all! Can they go on? Forgive? How to do that? Hearts are ripped in half. They feel dead inside; a part of them has died with their child's body. They feel nothing, just emptiness in their shock. It just can't be. The mother won't see her young boy's mischievous grin again or hear his childish giggle. The daughter's hugs that made the Daddy's heart sing – now no more. Oh Lord, tell them how to face each day. Help them God. She prays for Him to hold out His hand to all. Let His fingers grasp theirs and hold tight. He is the only hope, the only hope for all across the nation. Choose to believe. He wants to turn each tear into a diamond to shine in the dark blackness of this day. He will not forsake. Only through Him can they go on, can they see any light. Too much anger surrounds her in her Country.

As she ponders these events, she writes, trying to express the helplessness she feels:

Searching

A dark, deep sadness settles over the land.
It is almost Christmas: the celebrated Christian holy day.
Where is the brightness?
They come together and pray...all faiths represented;
Seeking solace and hope, searching.

Understanding does not come.
Darkness blinds them all.
They grope and stumble as they realize perhaps it
matters not "why"; the unanswerable question at least
in this existence.
The President of the land speaks wisely, "We must
protect our children.
If we get that wrong, nothing else matters."

What is she thinking, now?
The little ones are entrusted, a gift from God, for a short
while.
As they are guided to walk in God's love, they are
surrounded by love of others.

Can the shooter be forgiven, be loved?
Can the loved ones of the slain forgive? Can they not?
Can they not hate the sin, but love the sinner?

Can all do the same or do they let this evil rip love from their hearts as their children's lives were ripped away? Can they accomplish this momentous feat?

She thinks that this is the only choice, the only decision to make: to live out their lives in darkness, ever searching; or to find the Light... in forgiveness.

Her saddened spirit guides her to His word.

His word tells her that God is light. In Him there is no darkness. He who hates his brother has no light in him; but continues to stumble in the darkness, ever searching.

He, who stumbles often enough, will fall. Clear the path of hatred.

The young father holding his child, who survived, as he prepares to bury the one shot dead. He speaks to the citizens of his Country. Listen:

He chooses to forgive.

He prays for the confused gunman and for this young disturbed man's family. He tells of sympathy for the young man's parents and brother. He asks for them the release of the horrid grief they too must be feeling.

He is an example to all. He seems to be an angel, bringing the message of forgiveness and peace. Can one forsake their own deep sadness to think of others? She thanks their God for sending this model to all.

She pleads, Lord God, surround all with light. As light appears, a glimmer of hope emerges also. It grows, nourished by His love for all, And each one's love for another.

The Giver of so much mercy, in His love, helps all to follow. His strength allows each to forgive, as each makes the choice.

The darkness recedes and the brightness increases. Spreading His light into the darkness: from heart to heart, across the nation, across the world.

Lead all, Holy Spirit, for all to believe until they see their small child again someday. The moms and dads cry in anguish as He cries for all to return to Him. There is no choice but to seek His grace. This she thinks. This she knows. This she puts in her mind and memory. She prays for all.

She begs for herself the grace of God to totally forgive and forget just as Jesus does, any hurt, rejection, pain caused *to* and *by* her to others. She knows how difficult this battle is in her soul. If she can only learn and practice the kind of love that Jesus felt for all, the sinner and the victim. His love would be permeating her life, her world, her land. Help, Jehovah Rapha, her Healer. Help until the search is ended in His glory; as it is only through His strength that this can be accomplished. She knows that the Maker of all has forgiven all of the sins of those who ask: past, present, and future. How glorious and free she feels. Just like the kite she flew, as a child, in the windy sky; the lightness fills her.

Peace can come. Only with the help of the Lord will
anger leave. Hard work must sometimes be done to
search and find His peace. But it is always waiting
for each to walk in the sunlight of His word.

She did not understand the dimness enveloping her as she woke in the frosty morn. She could not explain it to herself; but it was real, heavy and dark. In her mind she was ruminating, too much, on what was happening in the world. Was she losing her way in the darkness of the day? What was she thinking? What thoughts were taking hold?

She Wept

She wept and wept and wept. All day long, as she put in the laundry, baked apple cinnamon bread, and set the table; she cried unceasingly for her country. As she drove through the splashing mist for groceries, tears formed deep, wet channels on her face. It's getting dark, so dark, so black.

Twenty, beautiful innocents shot multiple times in the Eastern part of her country. So stupid, so unnecessary! Twenty, beautiful innocents never to realize their purpose from God in this quickly snubbed out earthly life. A young American marine chained to the bed in a Mexican prison; for what offense? For nothing but taking a gun across the border that was shorter than the one for which he had a permit. The four ambassadors of good will and peace, in another part of the world, asking her government for more protection on 9/11, are shot, murdered. Oh, so very wrong. It makes no sense. Will the families and the citizens ever know how or why? The stock market dives, bringing distress to many. Congress stubbornly fights ideologies. Each side believing it is correct. No willingness to compromise is seen. Is it due to different goals? Are they hiding the real agendas? What is it that keeps them apart and unable to problem solve for the good of all? Each professes to want what's best for the country. The hurricane on the once beatific coast spreads ocean sand, like snow on lawns, as it left a terrific trail of destruction.

She wept and wept and wept. It was overwhelming to her. Her spirit was unable to bear the intense grief. Destruction and evil in her cherished country, so deep it takes away her breath. She tried to cast her care. She called out. She prayed. She rebuked. She asked; she sought; she knocked.

She wept. It didn't stop. She knew not what to do. She couldn't stop the torrent to her soul, just like the sleet and hail, hitting the windshield of the car as she drove. A sad day turned into a full, dark night. Where to turn? Just as the rain blinded her, flooding down the window; so her soul was covered in a deep, dark sadness. She prayed more and more, unceasingly. That's all she knew how to do. What choice was she making?

She fought for the grace to see God's face in all of this chaos. Is He even here? Have all turned so far away, too long, too deeply? Is He giving up on her beloved America? Taking back the covering of protection possessed since forming under Him? Or is there a purpose unseen to her eyes here on earth? She desperately wanted out of this enveloping darkness; to walk in His light again. How? How to get there?

Somehow, in the small sparkle of a very early Christmas light, blurred through the rain soaked window, He answered. She glimpsed hope. Gasping and grasping for life; He held her fingertips, guiding her hand on the wheel, bringing her home safely through the slushy dark streets.

Prayer brings hope. Prayer brings light into the darkest pit. Prayer with thanksgiving allows His light to slither into a crack, fill and then destroy the pit as she repents. She was not trusting. If she truly believes; then she realizes she must do the work of believing, which is trusting. This means totally submitting, not just partially.

It means realizing that not much is in her control; but rather all is in His. He will redeem. It means realizing that without Him, she can do nothing but with Him she can do all things through his strength. As the light seeps in, the hope, the peace, the joy comes ever so slowly to warm her heart. Giving thanks to Him spreads the balm throughout, assuages this rawness away to smoothness. Only the grace of thanks leads her back to the believing trust as she repents. She can truly cast her cares. She can feel them leave her mind, her thoughts, and her spirit. She stops and thinks about what she was thinking about!

She need not be afraid. She need not be dismayed. She weds her thoughts to his promises. She leans not on her own understanding; chooses not to let her heart be troubled. Yes, it is a choice! She thanks Him for this grace to see; thanks Him for sending that slight shaft of light to widen as she battles to reach out and hang onto His hand. Gasping, grasping, pulling, He lifts and carries her. Her heart is becoming lighter. Her spirit starts to soar as she continues to pray; as she continues to think about His faithfulness. Her country needs Him, her Christ, their Lord. Humbly she asks His blessing for His continued unmerited favor. His grace comes lavishly. For only by His grace can the confusion, anger, and deep wrenching sadness cease. Only by His light can the overwhelming darkness change. She trusts Him, her God, and her optimism returns and grows. She praises Him with thanksgiving! Humbly, she adores Him in this approaching holiday season.

> "But I call to the Lord, and the Lord saves me. Evening, morning, and noon I call out in distress and He hears my voice. He ransoms me unharmed from the battle waged against me."
>
> *-the NIV Bible, Psalm 55:16*

The gratitude for this fills her and brings the Light into the darkening evening. She has turned her thoughts to the characteristics and promises of Her God; through His strength.

And then again…the spirit of depression tries to attack. The battle continues in her thoughts, in her mind, in the supernatural. The war goes on.

A Devastating Storm Occurs

It happens again! Innocents are torn from their families. This time not by bullets: but by the uncontrollable wildness of nature. Teachers try to bring so many to shelter as the terrifying tornado blusters through the area. Blue skies have turned to gray, then green, then black. Deafening, detonating, exploding rage ruptures the town. The smothering, stifling storm blasts wide and long. Whining, wailing, whistling, shrieking, it extinguishes life as effortlessly as if one blew out a birthday candle. No more birthday gifts to be celebrated for and with these now dead children. Homes, schools, churches are lifted and smashed on concrete. Malls cave in and buildings crumble. Turbulence comes. Whirling through the land, the same kind of turbulence comes to her mind after the terror.

Then it's quiet. It seems oddly peaceful now as she looks at the sky. It's even sunny. But look at the rubble at her feet. Dark blackness is felt in the hearts of those remaining, as they search the mud for their lost child's body. She can't help but question "why?" This land is not the Sodom or Gomorrah of ancient times. Or is it? Is this what her country has become? Decidedly, definitely not! These children are not the sinners of old. Does man's extra, unnatural, scientific efforts cause such huge disturbance in the atmosphere that such a toll must be taken? Could it just be the thoughts and deeds of evil in the land causing this horrible disturbance in the atmosphere? If so, please forgive. She prays. Yes she knows that while He judges,

He does not send evil to His children – ever! Her God, her Jesus, with his death, burial and resurrection, sends only good gifts from above. This she knows by faith, only by faith. Again, she pleads for comfort and peace for the families torn asunder. She can rely on His truth spoken. She knows no other way. She comes to realize it is her choice as to what she thinks about: the evil in the world or His promises of unrelenting love and mercy. Which will it be? Anger turning to despair or hope? Reaching out in whatever way is possible. Is it fatalism or faith? She thinks about her choice.

> "I have loved you, my people, with an everlasting love; with unfailing love I have drawn you to myself. I will rebuild you…You will again be happy and dance merrily."
>
> *-the NLT Bible, Jeremiah 31:3*

Repenting to her God for all of the anxiety she felt about her Country, she releases what has caused her to be filled with such deep uneasiness. While it is important to know about current events, she had been "overdosing" on the news. She understood that it may often be slanted. So much of it was negative, she realized that most was totally beyond her practical control, or even impact. She didn't truly need to be filled with so much horrific detail everyday. It was causing the wrong kind of thinking in her brain! She knew the battle had to be fought supernaturally. Her time and energy could, perhaps even should, be occupied differently. She wants to trust, not distrust fretfully about God's providence. She chooses to grow her faith in trusting, in putting thoughts of His love and mercy in her mind.

Glistening Walk

Thoughts tumble through her mind like leaves falling from the autumn tree. Floating sideways, lifting, and then downward, finally landing. Sometimes making a decision; sometimes just wandering. Her emotions follow her thoughts, up and down and all around. She can guide her feelings; just simply by telling the thoughts to go, or to stay. She makes the decision on which she wants to keep, to think about. Such an immeasurably valuable strategy to know! Such an immeasurably valuable practice!

The black topped streets glisten and shine after the early morning autumn rain. The fallen leaves dot the still green, but yellowing grass. As she looks up at the tall trees, she sees gold, and orange, and bronze, and green, and yellow, and red—an endless abundance of hues and colors. She sees skinny, leafless branches reaching tall. They have lost their color but they are closest to the clouds.

Her eyes water as she talks to the Maker of heaven and earth. Then, like the streets, her heart shines after this early morning prayerful walk of thanksgiving. As she looks up, she sees now. Just like the bare branches reaching closer to heaven, she is there. She is reaching, reaching. Hope gives color to all. She is looking forward to a new miraculous day. All is well with her soul.

She thinks, then of her country, of recent unexpected terror, horrific acts of nature and of man. She lifts all to the Lord's care. She puts her trust in Him to solve the issues. There seems to be so very many now. She knows there is so much to be done, only through Him. She knows she must guard her heart and mind and feelings. She cannot stop. His love must be spread as it abounds. His purpose shall be realized. Yet she thinks of all the many "items on her plate;" facing her, her family, her community, and her country. She looks down at the dark, shiny blackness of the road beneath her feet – washed clean and glistening as He clears the path before her.

> "I have set the Lord always before me; because He is at my right hand; I will not be shaken. You have made known to me, the path of life; You will fill me with joy in your presence, with eternal pleasures at Your right hand."

> -the NIV Bible, Psalms 16:8, 11

She sees. She thinks. She receives peace.

She begins to see now more clearly that He is calling her to simply trust Him. Sometimes, it is not so simple but with Him it is possible. He is Lord of all and entirely more powerful than all the demons fighting for control over this world. She is starting to realize that her time could or should be spent more fruitfully in coming to know Him better in prayer. She is learning how to imitate the faith of a child again and again until she totally absorbs it. She replaces the negative doubting in her mind with truth in her God.

Prayer from Jeremiah

She wakes very early. She lifts, in prayer, all her loved ones, her friends, her church, her city, her country, her world. The Lord has spoken. "Come back to me and I will heal your wayward hearts." She labors to be in His rest, Oh Father. She praises Him. As the Lion of Judah comes to bring peace, the early light of dawn awakens. Her Father, who created light, lets her know deep in her spirit that this brightness is found in the face of Jesus Christ

She prays for light, for peace, for protection. Bring Light to those that don't understand unlimited love and mercy. Wake up, wake up the sleepy ones, the busy ones. Let all listen to Him. Let all in every land, hear of Him. Stop the wars, stop the fighting, and mostly stop the doubt. Labor to rest and wait in His peace, oh God. This is her thoughtful prayer. Help her to trust, Lord, always and as deeply as you love. Give her **your** wisdom, your compassion for all in need, for all suffering pain, for all in war torn lands. Let all seek and learn and help. Stop the weeping of your people. Heal wounds. Let her not be empty but full of peace and strength. Motivate all to help each other, to reach for and find His peace and strength.

Pray no more for those who rejoice in doing evil? Let the olive tree bear much fruit. Look at the deepest thoughts in her heart and mind, Oh God. Let her cringe not. Fill her with your love. Bring your light to her darkness and to that of others. Bring refugees to your complete safety. Stop the unspeakable child sexual slavery. Bring the sons and daughters in war torn lands home. Put an end to the rampant confusion regarding the truth.

You never abandon. All wait and trust with thanksgiving. Your Word sustains her through every battle. "Lord, you are her strength, her fortress, her refuge, in times of trouble." She is waiting for the light of dawn. It is coming. This she knows. This is a holy day, a Sabbath, a day to rest in your love. Thank You, Father.

> "Come back to me and I will heal your wayward hearts."
>
> *-the Bible NLT, Jeremiah 3:22*

> "For God who said 'Let there be light in the darkness'
> Has made her understand that this light is the brightness
> of the Glory of God as seen in the face of Jesus Christ."
>
> *-the Bible NLT, 2nd Corinthians 4:6*

Give her the assignment this day to honor Him and His word. Let His never ending grace and mercy spur her on to helping, then to rest with His peace as evening falls. He has for her a very special mission for this day. She wants to answer His call. Make it clear. Let her hear. For His glory, she thanks Him. She relies on her Father, on His will to be done; on earth as in heaven.

Her God hears her prayer and always answers. Her hunger for Him grows. She looks back at the path she has walked, the miles counted, the mountains climbed. She thinks about it. She thanks Him for the lamp onto her path. The Light was always there, even in darker times. He encourages her to skip and run in joy and freedom.

As the Rain Comes Down

Isaiah 55 in the Bible tells her that as the rain and snow come, so His word comes. In the Midwest, rain comes in all four seasons. Spring rains fall in torrents for subsequent days. It pours so ferociously that water is moving horizontally instead of vertically. Summer rains whisper softly in the evening on the fragrant blooms, making their aroma stronger and sweeter. Autumn rains bring winds to undress the trees tossing their colorful costumes all about. Winter clouds bursting bring icy slopes on which to skid or fall. Sometimes snow covers the earth quietly on a winter's evening, peaceful and beautiful. It may appear as an avalanche breaking free from a high mountain. It rolls down with power, sweeping everything in its way. The Lord goes on to tell her in Isaiah 53:10 that the rain comes to bring peace and productivity. So as she thinks His word comes in many different voices and many different ways.

Hearing Him guides her journey. She reflects on the evil, ever-present in this world. She thinks about the path His word has laid before her: the detours, the distractions, and the way back. How does she find her return trail? How does she hear Him? How does she know His promises? How can she understand all that He has told her? That's the question, the "million dollar "question. How can she ever hear all and even begin to understand? He teaches her to take one step at a time. He speaks to her mainly in His written word. He speaks to her through her trials and victories. He speaks to her through her friends, even strangers, as well as theologians' answers given in their teachings. Mostly He speaks to her in that quiet voice she hears in her mind as she asks for His thoughts. She feels His peace. The quietness that's heard as she listens, she recognizes as the Holy Spirit of Christ.

She tells of her concerns today. What is burdening her? He wants to take it. He does not want her to be troubled or distracted. She contemplates how to access that peace every day, every hour, every minute. How can she? It seems nearly impossible in her everyday world of hurrying, schedules, and demands. Only with His grace comes a supernatural ability to find it. His Spirit calms and guides her continually. He smiles down on her.

She looks forward so much to being in this presence every day. She has a new resolve to do anything to get there each morning. She realizes that its' not about doing; rather it's about being. Being His; being always at His feet. This becomes her daily agenda. She receives His help to stay there. She remembers her past experiences. Her most demanding and most rewarding vocation was having and guiding her children to adulthood. Teaching little ones how to read and write was next in energy needed and gratification earned. As also was educating others at the university level. For several years, she was active in various ministries: teaching Sunday school, tutoring reluctant learners, volunteering as room mother in her children's classrooms, assisting at church in the office, greeting food pantry, leading prayer groups, hosting bible study, offering healing prayers, writing and teaching prayer curriculum. It was worthwhile. It was blessed. She loved the people with which she worked and worshipped. As time passed, she was feeling the need for more, for different. She thought, "Ok, so what? What now?" She was always journaling, asking the Lord for direction. Yet she didn't see how she could squeeze in anymore. She began to understand more fully that it really isn't about earning His favor; but rather being His totally. She was asking God to use her as He willed.

She felt a deep yearning in her soul and spirit. She thought, at His urging she just needed to rest in Him. She took a hiatus from all the busyness. She spent time relaxing, enjoying the sunlight and sunsets going barefoot in the dew on the grass, summer's beautiful blooms. She grew ever more thankful and praiseful for these gifts from God. This spirit of thankfulness and peace grew within her as her closeness to God grew. She pondered all of His characteristics, so very many, so unbelievably great, that she cannot comprehend their value. Just love. The one quality she seems to know well. The one quality that He is continually teaching her how to reach more deeply: love.

She came to know that, as a matter of choice, she can live in His reality; as His word tells her that all of His promises are done and amen. She believes His word over what anyone says, or does, over whatever she hears or sees. "Come oh Lord, help me die to you" is her prayer. Help her come to the end of herself because her only hope is in you. She knows that she can do nothing without her God. The hope of glory is Christ, within her. With His strength, she can do all things. Really it's not her. He is doing all things through her as she finally and totally submits to His will more and more. It is all for His glory. Following His will for each day, in each circumstance, is where her peace lay. Spending more time with Him, worshipping Him, coming to know Him better; that's all He wants, to be close to her.

Her prayer life improved by leaps and bounds. She is beginning to understand more His mercy and grace. This is the age in which she lives. She came to realize this as she felt His presence. She never wanted to grieve Him again. The letter of the Law became less important to her. She started to understand more truly the phrase used throughout the Bible "by faith…" She continues reach, to strive to submit totally. Her peace is giving birth to a wondrous joy. It is not because of effort, but of submission. How busy she is doing His work is not the measure. Her wiliness to do His will is His answer. She begins to understand the joy of the Lord as she begins to trust Him more and more. She begins to understand only a small portion of His great love for her and others. She wants to please Him for Who He is, not so much for what He can do for her or give her. She wants only what He wants. The Holy Spirit is coming closer to her as the death of herself gives room for the life of the Spirit to take up residence within her. No effort, just peace and joy and hope for her future in spreading His kingdom. This is how she spreads His kingdom, not so much by witnessing but by becoming the witness in all of thoughts, words, reactions and actions. She interacts with only love, as Jesus did. Her tendency to judge others has decreased dramatically; she just smiles at them with encouragement as she comes to a better understanding of the truth that there is only one Judge. She begins each day with praise no matter what she is facing, how badly she might feel physically or emotionally. She doesn't ponder very long on symptoms she felt such as with the flu, being overtired, over anxious about various trials, large or small that her children and grandchildren were facing. She wasn't overly concerned with the evil going on in her larger world. These concerns are not hers. She gives them to Him. She has come to realize, that *anyway* she is diverted from the promises of God, brings doubt and anxiety. Rather, it's her daily goal to know His peace. It's been a long journey. It shall continue.

She thanks Him for the peace in her heart and mind so intense that it truly cannot be understood; only felt. She asks His help to never let her lose it. She knows now that what she chooses to think about is the thermostat of peace within her. And she thanks Him for sending His word, His insight to her as rain is needed by the drooping flowers and as the soft winter snow can give quiet to a soul. Peace and productivity are the result. She is jumping up and down with joy, just like a child receiving a new bike.

> "Oh people, the Lord has already told you what is good
> and this is what he requires of you: to do what is right,
> to love mercy, and to walk humbly with your God."

>   -the Bible, Micah 6:8

Now she prays that each and everyone come to Him, to the knowledge of His will for them. She wants the entire world to know His goodness, even as she continues on this journey. It would make this earthly life so much easier to bear for each. Asking for, receiving the faith of a little child is a choice.

"Let the morning bring me word of your unfailing
Love, for I have put my trust in you. Show me the
way I should go, for to you I lift up my soul."
-NIV Bible, Psalm 143:8

PART IV

Winter: A Time of Special Beauty A Time to Celebrate Death

The woods call for her to come, walk, to share their peacefulness.

"In the depth of winter, I finally learned that there was in me an invincible summer."

-Albert Camus

The Yellowed Field

The yellowed field turns bluish-white.
The snowfall makes it new and bright.
Quiet, peace so intense,
One's heart bursts forth with joy.
The black branches stretch and reach and shadow.
Yet through them, light wins the battle.

"He gives snow like wool;
He scatters the frost like ashes,
He casts forth His ice as fragments;
Who can stand before His cold?
He sends forth His word and melts them."

-the NIV Bible, Psalms 147: 16-18

And as she grows older, she becomes closer to Him; as she comes to know Him better. She seeks that invincible summer, that brightness of the summer's sun all year long. She thinks about if she can find it in this life. A long road is behind her, just as long or longer ahead remains? She longs to live only for Him each day, always for her God, her Jesus. This is her purpose in being: to worship Him.

She Thinks About Death

"It is not the length of life; but rather the depth of life."

-Ralph.WaldoEmerson

What is the depth of life? What does "the depth of life" mean? There is so much about death that she does not understand. The Word of God, which is true, tells her that there is an appointed time for each. It also tells her that each will be given a long and satisfying life. She often wonders if one has a voice or a vote on when the final day arrives. Perhaps? She's heard about instances when two people are stricken with the same disease; each in a very similar physical condition; with same secondary factors influencing their outcomes. One dies; yet one survives. Why one and not the other? Doctors attribute it to the will to live, or even to a miracle. Others attribute it to prayer. Still others attribute it to faith. She has read books about those few pronounced dead; who come back to write about their experience. Do they understand the depth of life better now? Did they come to understand it while they were still alive? Did they even think about it? Most likely they did. There is much concerning death that one is not to know. It was planned this way. Has it anything to do with free will; with the ability to make choices after thinking, discerning what life and its' depth may mean? Does time spent in the presence of her God deepen her life?

All she really knows is that she will die…someday. Everyone will. No one doubts this truth. Many avoid thinking about their death. Most avoid talking about it. Only God knows about all of the mystery surrounding the time and place. She knows she must trust her God. He sent His Son to save the world; there was no other answer. That's a profound mystery; not meant to be understood, while in this worldly existence.

She's not afraid to die. She just doesn't want to leave her loved ones yet. She feels for them deeply; she knows she will be missed. She doesn't want to cause them sadness. She could even look forward with great anticipation to dying if it weren't for this fact: the suffering of those left to live out their lives until called. She knows she must trust her God. She knows that death is really a cause to celebrate. She also knows that it is a time of mixed emotions for those present, those remaining.

She knows the source of death: the evil one. But knowing that doesn't help the understanding because there is so much, much more. She sees that this evil one who comes to steal life can come like a thief in the night, uninvited. He can come silently, quickly, totally unexpected as a heart grows to weary to beat any longer. It can come violently with much chaos; the finality of the gun shot followed still by the screaming of those witnessing and the shrieking of the sirens. In what seems like a moment, the stillness deafens. Death can even come as it is asked for, sought after by the person in indescribable pain or anguish; or by the loving caregiver watching such agony. When this happens, she understands that the dark face of the angel of death is welcomed; knowing that as believers the sting of death is truly the last victory. It brings a new beginning, a new life with no pain, suffering, anguish or tears. She truly cannot comprehend why a young mother dies and leaves her little children to someone else with such a gaping emptiness; that it is often never filled. Young children die and leave bewildered parents, wounded so deeply, so full of misunderstanding and confusion; that they sometimes cannot even love each other any longer. At such times the love of Christ may be buried beneath the weeping of the grieving. She knows only that she must trust her God. God is the Author of Life Eternal, not death. Yet One who knows all the "whys, when's, and wherefores."

She knows what she knows: that there is a beautiful afterlife, hers for the seeking: to each and everyone. So wondrous is this time of eternity after earthly life, beyond anything that she could ever imagine. This is why she has no fear. This is why she welcomes death; of seeing others again, already gone before her; of actually meeting even more personally her God. As she thinks about it, she begins to grow, in her trust of her God's timing. Only He is meant to know the reason for the timing. She thanks Him for this grace filled insight.

The deep sadness and confusion felt by those left, she understands partially, but never totally. Shouldn't it truly be a time for celebration? Shouldn't the focus be not on the grieving but on the gift that the loved one receives in dying? *Can* it be on that focus? Only with the strength of God, as the grieving raise their hands in the sanctuary to give praise, can the celebration begin. She waits patiently, looking forward to the vapor of her life dissipating someday. She prays that those left will remember her with fondness and love, not pain; as they revel in happy memories and the knowledge that she is waiting for them in eternity. She prays that they will understand the joy in which she is now immersed. She trusts her God, who knows the future; for it is He Who orders each day.

> "...for when our perishable earthly bodies have been transformed into heavenly bodies that will never die---
> then at last the Scriptures will come true:

Death is swallowed up in victory.

O death, where is your victory?

O death, where is your sting?"

For sin is the sting that results in death, and the law gives sin its power.

How we thank God, who gives us victory over sin and death through Jesus Christ, our Lord!"

-the NLT Bible, 1 Corinthians: 15:54 - 56.

Law gives sin its power? Then the mercy and grace of Jesus Christ give death its celebration. It is by faith, that one is saved to reach the victory, the celebrated Eternal Life. Help her Lord; help each Lord, not to be so consumed with temporal life here on earth that it becomes the only reality, or even the most important or valued reality. Your promise for eternal life is that which is to be believed in, to be sought. She needs His assistance to fight this battle of faith, at times of mixed emotions: sadness and joy. Only He, her God, can lead her, lead each, out of darkness into the Light, as seen in the face of Jesus Christ. For this insight, she will always raise her hands in praise, always eternally.

"He, who aims for heaven, gets earth thrown in. He, who aims for earth, loses both."

-C.S.Lewis

Premature death, whether before birth, or at a young age is a mystery that cannot be grasped. Sometimes it is so obvious to the observer; when human choices bring about an early death. But the reason for a young innocent leaving too soon; she cannot comprehend. She realizes that there is much hidden from her and others. She accepts the wisdom of God, with the faith of a child; not understanding, but forcing herself to say, as she thinks, "Ok, my God, only you know the future. I surrender."

The Young Mother Mourns

The tiny baby opens his eyes and glances around. He came into this world too early. Will he stay? His eyelids flutter. He softly closes them in everlasting sleep and peace. What unspeakable joy is his now! No trials to ever bear; only knowing love during his short life and now greater love forever.

What unspeakable pain this leaving causes the young mother's mourning. She sobs deeply through the dark night. Every heart-wrenching tear of the first-time parents is caught. Their brokenness in this moment causes weeping with them; as those around them witness the agony felt. Understanding eludes. Their deep despair is recognized. They cannot carry the pain any longer. Only God knows what sadness from which this little son was saved. Only God can heal this deep wound of the heart.

The young mother raises her hands in the holy sanctuary of their home as she knows that God is somehow, somewhere near them. She believes that her wrenching prayers offered are never left unanswered. Each prayer is answered by the One who knows the future. This precious blessing, this gift from God was snatched too soon by Satan; meaning evil; but it failing to be evil; as the early death causes wondrous miracles instead.

The everyday lives of the young parents live out their destiny on earth, day by day. A small measure of peace and joy, ever-increasing, comes to each day by day, as they thank God for this angel in heaven. The mom and dad see him guarding and helping his yet-to-be brothers and sisters, even his own yet-to-be spiritual children and grandchildren, generation after generation. The mother and father kneel in adoration as they open their hearts and hands to receive His faithfulness, not understanding but receiving the strength to go on each day, to help comfort others in this troubled world. This baby will guide the heart and hands of mom and dad to receive from Christ. This baby will speak encouragement through them to others in pain; to guide others to receive from Christ. All of this is for His glory; not to further the plan of the demon.

As the shattered hearts are patched through prayer and grace, the sunlight filters into the darkness. What is heart-breaking, God turns into a miracle of giving joy and peace and comfort to others. The young parents are surrounded in prayer themselves. They, then, surround others in need; weeping with them as tears become prayers. They help others seek Him, not always, not ever understanding why. Above all else, they thank Him for the blessing of this angel, held in their arms, for just a little while; now being held in eternal blessedness. As the mom and dad grow and become parents and then grandparents; more joy comes to them, now, in so many different ways. Though there is mourning in the night; the morning brings joy.

She ponders what her God has told all…

> "O Lord, God of her salvation, She has cried out to you
> day and night. Now hear her prayer, listen to her cry. She
> is forgotten, cut off from your care, each day she begs for
> your help, O Lord; she lifts her pleading hands to you for

mercy. Of what use are the dead to Your miracles! Do the dead get up and praise You? Oh Lord, she cries out to You. She will keep on pleading day by day."

-the NLT Bible, Psalm 88:1, 2, 5, 6,9,13

That's how she feels. She asks him for help, or inspiration, for His peace.

"Trust me in your times of trouble, and I will rescue you,
And you will give me glory."

-the NIV Bible, Psalm 50:15

Help all, Oh holy God, as unexplained death in the earthly life is faced; as that unknown path is traveled. Stumbling may occur; but wandering ones are not lost.

"It is good to give thanks to the Lord,
To sing praises to the Most High.
I sing for joy because of what You have done."

-the NIV Bible, Psalm 92:1, 4

And to continue to give thanks for what He continues to do. She begins to realize that often, the only way to open the door is to turn the key of praise. She uses it to open the way to joy again. This brings her to the peace that truly is beyond her understanding. She finds ways to spread this peace to others. Joy is the result. She thanks Him for this insight into His word, His will.

Her good friend lost her husband and soul mate to cancer. Knowing this happens all too often, she is filled with empathy as she imagines her friend returning to the empty house after the funeral on that sunny day. No dark clouds or rain outside, but such feelings inside, only a deep sadness and loneliness exist.

Her Friend, Alone and Sad

It was a life well lived.
As his wife laid him in the grave,
A warm and sunny afternoon
Many family and friends with her.
To say goodbye until they meet again.
And now, her friend goes home and sits alone,
To look out at the yard he loved so much.
He is not here; he is missed.
No one can believe that he is gone.
She is alone and she is so sad.

He is out of pain.
A meaningful ending,
To the life of fullness of joy and love.
He is restored and healthy once again.
But the widow is alone and she is so sad.

Somehow, it isn't right, Dear Lord.
Why? Why did it have to be?
The widow asks for understanding.
"Couldn't he have waited and
We could somehow leave together?

A place that you prepared for him,
And one for me: as well?"
Sometimes, the one left just wants to go there now.
To join her love: to stop the sadness.
Knowing that the end was coming: the end
To all his suffering: helps but little.
As more suffering is left now
The widow is all alone and she is sad.

Watching as the shadows lengthen,
Like the vice that's tightening her heart.
Can she go on? *How* can she go on?
The tears trickle down as she ponders in silence
Dark and deepening depression
She is so alone and sad.

She must go on she tells herself. She simply *must*.
But oh so very, very difficult! Impossible.

She will go on.
She has no choice.
But *only* with the strength of God;
Added to the strength of the memories they shared.
But such happiness gets lost on this sunny day,
Looking out the window at the yard he loved so much.
She is alone and sad.
Will her pain end soon? Will it end at all?
It must. It shall. *Only* with her Lord,
Thanksgiving is offered for hope as she
Chooses to dwell on the eternal life
Without pain.
Traded for the temporary life.

They shall be together again.
She is alone for now;
But not so sad.

"My soul shall be joyful In the Lord; it shall rejoice in his salvation."

-the NLT Bible, Psalms 25:1

The young son's physical life is snuffed out in a tragic accident. Again she ponders the feat of not understanding the "why"; but the necessity of accepting, what seems to have no reason. For this is the only way she can demonstrate her trust. The incomprehensible remains just that – seemingly totally senseless to her. She does not waiver in the truth that there is One who knows much more than she; who understands much more than she. She walks this tragic road with two different friends, each losing their teen-age sons. One many years ago, one this past year, was torn from his family. She weeps with them, wonders with them, and asks why with them.

A Death Too Soon: She Asks Why

The Psalms Answer

The Psalms are calling out to the mother in time of great trial, deep sorrow. The mother feels forgotten, abandoned, cut off from her God. Unspeakable sadness has thrust her down into the lowest, darkest pit. The tears fall continually on her face. Is her God angry with her for some reason? Is that why this sudden death happened? Why, why, oh Lord, this tragedy? If only the clock could be turned back a couple of minutes on that dark night. If only the squealing of tires could have been silenced more quickly; before the impact. If only the crash that took the young man's life, had been avoided. If only, if only you, God, had heard her prayer she laments; a miracle would have occurred. Weren't you listening?

In anger the words of the psalm, are spoken, "Those in the grave cannot declare God's unfailing love to others. Those in the place of destruction cannot proclaim His faithfulness. Those in the darkness cannot speak of His miracles." These words of David echo her feelings. The bereft mother questions what appears to be His rejection of her family and of herself; as their request for a miracle in the emergency room that night, appears to go without answer. Did He hear their desperate cry? Did He even listen? Her son, on the brink of manhood and independence, has been taken away from them. Only deep grief remains where once there was joyful light. There is only darkness now. The unending tears from her eyes and from her heart make it so very difficult for her to see any explanation for this seemingly senseless death. The gloom of despair fills the rooms of her house; and the souls of those left in the dull dwelling. She knows not what to do, where to turn, what to say and even what to think. She places one foot in front of the other as she walks out endless days of misery and misunderstanding. Sometimes, she cannot even pray. She just can't comprehend why all the prayers for a miracle healing were not heard. She trusted His Word. She wants so badly to have her path set straight again to feel once again the joy of the morning sun. But is that even possible after this horrific loss?

She prays now with closed eyes, blindly. She cries out, "Help me. Where, oh where is your faithfulness? Let me rest in You, Lord." The only possible way to bring light into her darkness must be in His word. But she can't find it. She cannot feel the comfort of His peace and love. Only He can help her in her search. Release her from the pain, the torment. Come quickly. This becomes the prayer. She pleads to Him to keep confusion from her friend; to give her His wisdom. It is so difficult, so oppressive.

Understanding the unexpected death of a loved one, especially a young person, is not only unacceptable, it is impossible. It is beyond the human mind and emotions. To try to explain or reason why this early death occurred is futile and totally incomprehensible. Is the reasoning mind stopping one's journey of drawing nearer to God; of feeling His comfort and peace?

The once strong cord between the mother and her God is now a sliver of a silver thread. Will it break? Somehow, this mother holds onto it. She knows not how. She tries to draw nearer to God; as she places one hand in front of the other, pulling closer. She grips as tightly as possible to avoid falling backwards into the muck of despair. The strength of the cord exists, even in its frail appearance. She knows that she will never be fully severed from her Master regardless of this grief-filled time; as she knows also that she will never be fully severed from her son, gone from her for now. The silver link is strengthened as it is wrapped in the gold of His love.

The gleaming link of the chain connecting to her God is strengthened as her unending-tormented prayer for relief continues. This is all she knows to do. Lord, how long will this go on? How long will He hide from her, she wonders. Somewhere her faith in Him is there as His love reaches down to the mother. He is with her. He has told her that He will never leave her, never forsake her. She begins to fully believe again, to stop the tormented questioning.

Then the psalmist tells her that God's faithfulness is God's very character. He crushes the great sea monster created by her tears: the chaos in her heart and soul. His throne is founded on the two pillars of righteousness and justice. Mercy abounds and connects. He did not come for the righteous; but rather to those in great need, those lost. He hears and answers; He refreshes the spirit of the mother. He tells her that her enemies will not get the best of her. He renews her as she dwells in His word. She thinks. She ponders. She comes to wonder at it all. He beats down her adversaries as the command is given, "Destroy them!"

Through His strength she perseveres to finally hear His call. She listens attentively. She binds the bewildering question of "Why this sting of death? Where is your truth, oh God?" These questions she does not linger on any longer. In her grieving, she comes to discern the source of such pondering as the same evil one that took the young man's life. She does not want to cooperate in the distraction that the dark one tries to send. She knows deep down in her glimmer of faith in God; that only He knows the future. Help her to remember how short her own life is, how futile this temporary human existence is. Guide her as her whole life becomes worship – everyday a prayer, all day long, bringing Him glory. As the Psalm tells, no one lives forever, all will die. No one escapes the grave. Her boy is in heaven with Him; perhaps saved from different harm? This she knows as He who had begun a good work in him is faithful to finish. This Truth, only, gives her fleeting solace.

Another following psalm tells her to live in His shelter. She finds rest in His shadow. He alone is her Refuge from every trap. As she strikes her foot on the stone of wondering and wandering; He takes her hand. No evil will conquer her; not even this unimaginable worldly death. Her God has plans for her future. He gives her a new spirit, a new purpose to walk in His way and His will each day. She is renewed and refined by His power. He is her rock. There is nothing but goodness in Him. She determines not to stumble. She will always miss this son: thinking of him, remembering his smile, his laugh, his love. His birthdays will not come; neither his earthly death date, without some grievous remembering. His appointed time seemed too early to all but she trusts in the Creator that someday she may clearly see. They all may clearly see. Her heart will always hurt; but now she feels an overwhelming peace that He is in control. On these special occasions, she will praise and honor her God. She seeks now His will for her remaining days as one's life is so short until He calls each home. He has good plans for her future. For now, she trusts. Trust is not only a belief, it is an action.

Come, sing to the Lord. Let her worship and bow down. Let her come before Him with thanksgiving for rescuing her. Let her sing songs of praise again. Lord, take her there. Fill her spirit as her remaining life becomes a powerful, prayerful praise to her God; as she finds her way out of days of immeasurable sadness. Let her spread the news of the Lord's greatness as believers and non-believers alike wait and watch as her joy in living comes back.

She ponders...perhaps her peace will come. She thinks much. She knows now that it will come. She knows not the details but she learns to trust again.

> "O Lord, God of her salvation,
> She cries out to you day and night.
> Now, You hear her prayer, listen to her cry.
> She is forgotten, cut off from your care.
> She is thrust down to the lowest pit, into the darkest depths.
> Each day she begs for your help, O lord;
> She lifts her pleading hands to you for mercy.
> Of what use to the dead are your miracles!
> Do the dead get up and praise you?
> O Lord, She cries out to you.
> She will keep on pleading day by day."

> *-the NIV Bible, Psalm 88:1, 2, 5, 6, 10, 13*

How to find it? Ask and she will receive? She has been asking. Persevere? Is this the only option available? As all of her sisters in Christ come to pray for her as well for she knows that there is great power in united prayer. Even they question themselves, "Have they done enough, listened enough, checked in with her enough, prayed enough?"

> "For, if two or more of you come together in my name,
> there I am with you."

> *-the NIV Bible, Matthew 18:20*

It is oh so difficult for her. She is surrounded in
prayer unrelentingly. Their prayer for her:
"I lay my whys before your cross,
In worship kneeling, my mind too numb for thought;
My heart beyond all feeling,
And worshipping, realize that I in knowing you
Don't need a why."

-Ruth Graham Bell, My Laughing Fire.

She perseveres. Her sisters and brothers in Christ join her in prayer. A prayer of thanksgiving arises as the Holy Spirit touches her; as she gives of herself to others all around; until she sees her son again in eternity forever. Thank You, God Father.

She knows and believes deeply the words of her God that He who began a good work in this child will complete it. He is God. She thinks about the other boy taken just as suddenly, at about the same age.

Finding the Way

The son was taken in his teen years, the two weeks of his high school graduation festivities. This tragic accident that killed him almost killed his mother's ability to function; her will to live. Her story is told on paper beautifully as the mother authors the story of her travel. She takes the reader on her journey from total brokenness to being surrounded in the unconditional love of God in her book, Above The Valley. There are so many jewel-like facets on the pathway that glitter now in the sunlight of her living. One feels her deep pain as reading her thoughts. One feels her joyful peace as she comes from the valley of deep sadness to the top of the mountain in victorious love.

With the loss of a loved one, especially an unexpected early death; a chasm appears, between what one knows to be God's truth and how one actually feels, that is immeasurably wide. Can it be breached? Her unimaginable broken-heartedness, and sometimes torment described in detail, helps one understand her pain. No one is immune or protected from this possibility as death is the destiny of all. Only the timing differs.

This horrific, episodic loss can help others experiencing a similar robbery, the same or a similar destruction. What she describes, focusing on great difficulties, has been felt by others. Depending on one's reaction, one's grieving process, God can and will use such an experience to allow the grieving to reach out and help others climb their own momentous mountain – an ever, ever slow, often painful ascent. Whatever occurs to cause great difficulty, deep sorrow can be the plane to heights unknown. Or such a defeat can maim, crush or even kill. What makes the difference? The reactions based on one's beliefs point the way traveled. The reactions that can light the roadway or keep it in darkness so that no relief, no victory is ever realized.

Where does one look for and find this help, understanding, and peace? The mother shows us in each step she takes up the mountain from the valley to the summit. Trusting the God who knows the future clears the path. Perhaps saving this young person from intolerable pain in his earthly life? And saving those loved ones around him from the same? Yet knowing the Author of Eternal Life; there is much hidden; much that isn't to be known until eternity. Peace still comes; His peace that goes beyond any understanding tragedy in this life.

> "Because of our faith, Christ has brought us into this place of highest privilege where we now stand, and we confidently and joyfully look forward to sharing God's glory."

> *-the NLT Bible, Romans 5:2*

She reached and felt the peace that is greater than
her understanding. That peace is from God.

Then there is the destruction of the demon named "addiction". Reason flees as control is given over, not to good, but to evil. She witnesses this mother watching the young man, her son, make the devastating choice time after time as his will is suffocated into bondage of alcohol and drugs, a different kind of "death".

The Evil Demon

The mother is lost in the dismal heaviness. She searches for answers. Where did this demon come from? What happened? Why? What is the answer? Is there an answer? What can she do to dispel it? What should she do?

She thinks in her troubled state. Was it something she said or did? Something she didn't say or do? Did she love and nurture him enough? Did she do so in the "right" way? Did she neglect to love openly when she corrected or disciplined this boy? Did she not explain enough? Why is he now making such self-devastating choices? Was it the result of an unrequited young love as he grew into manhood? Was it the horror of war? Of picking up body parts and placing them gently into black plastic bags? Was it the quick financial success he gained as a stock broker in his young professional life? Did wisdom flee as the god of money succeeded? What happened to his soul to turn him into a shadow of himself? The bright one: that was filled with goals to perform and achieve? The bright one who knew his God: but seems to have lost sight. No longer is he the conqueror.

Now he is filled with harmful substances that numb his deep; secret pain. Illegal substances at illegal levels create in him a dull, dank darkness. His goal now has become a daily fix; the only way he knows how to put one foot in front of the other each morning; until he collapses in a stupor and sleeps in numbness. Total dysfunction, shutting down of his reasoning power results as he escapes the gut-wrenching demon showing him a reality he cannot watch or survive.

"What happened?" she whispers. She doesn't understand, just doesn't get it. "How did this beautiful, productive child, reaching God-given potential as a young man become this sorry mess?" He is so lost in his created pit of mucky pain, that he cannot pull himself out.

He cannot help himself; except to fast talk his way out of rehabilitation programs. He knows the answers the professionals want to hear. Even the answers to the doctors when committed involuntarily by the court; he says the right words to free himself from barred windows and locked doors. This talent of fast talking is really no help to him at all. He seeks his own unique barred windows and locked doors as he sinks into the pit more deeply. He can only help others like himself by making deals for the next drink or the next snort to take each higher out of reality into the state of unfeeling deadness. He doesn't have to think to fight his demons, to wage the war he cannot seem to win: this waste of talent. His ability to think is dulled. The destruction of his soul and body and will to live takes him over everyday. The power and authority given by Christ is hidden now. Accomplishing all things through God's strength is forgotten.

The mother watches as she sits in her car parked near the homeless gathering in the woods. She witnesses the unrelenting pull on her loved child-man into the black evil world of alcohol and drugs. His brightness dims. His words make no sense. His eyes darken blankly. His half-smile is fake, almost demonic. He doesn't want to live; doesn't have the strength to shiver through another frosty night sleeping under trees. He tries to warm himself by the fire, almost stumbling into it crunching over hot twigs and branches.

He takes the blanket she offers; wrapping it tightly around him to keep out the snowy, dampness all around him. Unknowingly, he tries to keep out the world of tears he sees and feels as his mother turns and trudges away slowly, sadly. She is surrounded in a dismay of massive proportions; as she walks into the dark trees.

Again, she asks "Why? Why is this happening?" She has tried to right him, to support him, to talk with him, to guide him, to drive him to treatment, to pray him to better choices. Nothing helps. He rejects it all, preferring his own dismal destiny of daily decisions leading to darkness. What does one do when she has done everything she possibly could to help?

She tries to pray; to trust her grown child, now a wasted man, to her God. The father of the boy prays; as do the sister, brother, and friends. Diversion only seems to help her. She tries to have fun. She goes to lunch, to shop, to spend time with friends. But the coldness, always there, is tightening its grip on her heart and soul.

Carrying this strain of her broken heart, the mother's body weakens. It is much too heavy for her to keep. She cannot help to ease his pain or take it from him. He will not give it up. Her repeated attempts, time after time after time, to rescue him wear her down. Total absorption with his problem life now becomes hers. Depression closes in on her. Her thoughts turn dark as she plans his actual funeral in her mind. She starts to believe that her son's choices are numbering his days on this earth; hastening his physical death.

Through prayer, she comes to realize that a total, complete, eternal submission of this son to the forces-that-be is necessary. Good or evil, what is the choice? Which will it be? This is not her decision to make. Oh, if only it were she wishes. She understands with more clarity now that it was nothing she said or did; didn't say or do. She realizes that his addiction really is trading away the future so that he can feel ok right now as Catherine Hyde Ryan describes in her book, "Don't Let me Go." Letting this boy go is the only answer. Giving this young man to her God is what she hears when she prays: "Detach." She must. *Her* efforts at fixing him are fruitless. She must release him totally. She must consider him… well… dead. The death of a soul seems to come slowly often with more pain than physical death. As one falls into the yawning abyss of hurt, misunderstanding, frustration because of events in one's life, anger and finally the deep sadness of giving up of one's mind to the demons results. She understands now what she may never totally understand; what only God knows as He knows her child's heart. Her grown child, her son, no longer exists to her. She places him completely, forever in the hands of Christ, who loves him even more than she. Christ, the One who has only good plans for the future of her child will take over his future. As she prays, she asks for God's strength. It is so difficult to follow the wise words she hears from her God.

As she stands on God's promises, her health begins to improve. She recaptures her thoughts from the evil one possessing the son; which is now trying to steal the mother as well. She knows she can only achieve this momentous task through the strength of Christ who gives so generously when asked. She turns away from the vacant-eyed gathering around the fire. She turns away from this child-man toward the destiny God has chosen for her. She begins to lean, to trust. Her battle is to choose to believe that her child is in God's hands; that God knows the future. He can and does take care of all. His will shall be done.

She fills her mind with the mind of Christ and her day with the will of Christ. She does this with His Word and by His grace. Her joy returns only as she submits to trusting her God. Everyday, many times each day, she thinks about the word and work of Christ. She fights her battle to victory. She knows not of the whereabouts of the "dead" son. No cause for alarm to her, as she comes to truly understand that he belongs totally and eternally now to his Creator. Her daily labor brings fruit instead of tears and unproductive thoughts of total sadness. Peace and joy surpassing her understanding come to her. She fights to keep it; to not let any thought steal her joy. She is taking the huge step across that giant, canyon of belief in God to total belief of God's word: admitting that the boy is no longer alive to her. God gives her a renewal of spirit. He won't give up on this lost boy. Neither will she. The son, dead to the mother, is in the palm of Christ fills her with light as she comes to know that all is well. She praises God. She thanks Him.

> "You have been speaking to me, Lord, about my children (and grandchild). You loaned him (them) to me for a season. Now I am to take my possessive, managing hands off strictly off. You will perfect him (them) them in your way and in your timing. Years ago you began this work. It is your business to complete what you start. You have promised that you will. It is as good as done."

> *-Catherine Marshall as quoted in "Dear God, It's Me and It's Urgent." Parentheses are the words found in original poem; different pronouns substituted by author.*

Only by forcing her own thoughts from the dark of the devastation, the answer to her prayer comes. He may bring wisdom to the subject or He may bring the peace without understanding. Whichever, she is able to thank Him; to give Him glory.

Trust

The snow is so heavy and thick that it is weighing down the sturdy pine branches. It creates a drape of seclusion, a beautiful picture. She watches the huge flakes floating down in mesmerizing silence. The sun breaks through the branches. A clump of snow finds itself wandering down to the white covered earth; a scene, filled with peace, to record and remember.

She thinks of herself, sometimes weighed with worry. Sometimes she cries in her spirit for others' challenges. Heavy and burdened, is there a way to show her love? Often times, no, not really. She prays for them. Early death, unexpected death, the loneliness of those left are unsolvable for this moment. Circumstances, causes and effects are way beyond her reach. But these things are not beyond the reach of her God.

Rather, look up. Labor always, in trust, so that she enters into His rest. This is what He tells her. Her only work is to trust Him, His word, His promises. Then she rests in His peace. Submit. Depend on Him; for she is told that He who has started a good work will complete it. The sun shines brightly. There is no heaviness now. The thick snow falling provides the firm basis on which to tread. This place of seclusion becomes a sanctuary for her soul.

Wake up her dozing soul, oh Lord. Bring wisdom, compassion for all in need, suffering pain, those in war-torn lands. Seek and learn. Stop the weeping. Heal the wounds. Empty anger, bitterness. Fill with peace and strength. Let the olive branch bear much fruit. Bring light to the darkness. Waiting for the light of dawn; knowing it is coming. This is a holy day, a Sabbath. This is a day to rest.

Bring those left to a knowledge and understanding of the beauty of earthly death: a passing into another life of complete total deep joy; never to suffer pain, loss, desolation of any kind. Bring those left the joy of memories and the realization of the shortness of temporal life. Bring those left the peace of the heavy snowfall, at first frightening, but then of the deepness of His love for all.

> *"And so, God willing, we will move forward to further understanding."*

-the NLT Bible Heb 6:3

The concept of eternity is incomprehensible, isn't it? The joy of heaven is also; as is the horribleness of hell. Many deny the lake of fire's existence. All she can wonder is; "What if you're wrong?" Pray for the truth to come. Surround all in love and wisdom, as they make the choice for Truth. Eternity is to big a gamble to not be sure.

His body succumbed to the dreaded disease. Her brother-in-law didn't live to see his first grandchild but she knows that he is at a much better place. He is watching his beloved family from above He is eternally happy with a joy much greater than if he were here.

A Death in the Family

The low murmuring manages to drown out the silence of sadness. Every so often, she hears the familiar laugh of this youngest sibling; as memories are shared in softened voices. She watches her youngest sister circulate among those who came to grieve with her. Surrounded by the children of the husband lying in eternal peace, this wife and mother circulates among the friends. No more pain, no more treatment, no more emergency trips to the hospital as all for him on earth is finished. The sister-in-law thinks back just a couple of days ago when she stopped to see him. Drawn, thin, and tired looking, he was waiting for his physical healing miracle. The dog is barking loudly and constantly, registering anger at what only the animal may sense: the nearness of death. It is difficult to speak to each other above this continual complaining noise. She wants to encourage him. He's too young to leave his family, to never see his grandchildren. A few days pass. It's too late. She woke that night of receiving the final news, after sleeping only a few hours. How she regretted not bravely asking if he was ready to meet Jesus when she visited with him last. She searched for every scripture pleading for deep understanding of "unless a man be born again of the Spirit...," Only one way to reach heaven. She wept in her confusion of the loss. Which loss of him or of Him, or both; she knew not. She knelt in the dark night with only moonlight shining and asked for revelation.

"He who began a good work in him will bring it to completion."

-the NIV Bible. Philippians 1:6

She seems to understand now that her brother-in-law is in God's hands, in His presence. She realizes it's not up to her. He is God's chosen; her heart tells her. She knows that his prayers were answered: that he did, in fact, receive his miracle of eternal Life. This miracle cannot be understood by her human mind, only her heart. Such concepts are incomprehensible because of their tremendously unfathomable size. As is her God.

She came to peace. She knew that he knew his God who opened the gates. She came to the realization that the fruit of this man be his children to carry on. At last she slept to face the memorial. At last she was able to offer her questioning nephew, hope in her prayer and encouragement in her words through the inspiration of the Holy Spirit. Her God is only and totally Love and compassion. She glorifies her God.

"The Lord my God will enlighten my darkness."

-the NLT Bible, Psalm 18:2

She searches and finds Light in knowing Jesus Christ.
She thanks Him for enlightening her darkness.

As she ponders these physical deaths around her and even her own, she is beginning to understand the joy unspeakable that is to be found in heaven. This life on earth has moments and glimpses of just a shading of this immeasurable happiness. She knows that it now belongs to many forever and that it will belong to her forever some day. She begins to see the celebration of death.

And When She Dies

At the age when more friends start leaving this world for the next, one's mortality becomes more real. She thinks about her own. How, when will she die? He tells her, in His word, that He will grant her a long and satisfying life. She believes His word; not because she always understands it. No rather, just because it is His word. While she looks forward to heaven; she doesn't feel ready yet. Has she completed His work? Has her purpose, set out for her by God, before she was born, been accomplished? She is thinking about the "how" and the "when" of it all.

Of course she wants to leave painlessly. Doesn't everyone? Of course, she wants to leave surrounded by those she loves and those who love her. Doesn't everyone? Bittersweet but hopefully after a life well lived-as well as can be in her imperfect soul in an imperfect world. Will she hear "Well done, good and faithful servant."?

Will she be given time to say good bye? In the past she has stayed away from saying goodbyes. As when her brother went off to fight the war in Vietnam; she didn't go to the airport. She didn't want to experience possible images of him not returning; or returning in a flag-draped wooden box. Or when her Mom was in the fight of a massive stroke; she stayed away. She was afraid to go to the hospital because of receiving chemo at that time. Her immune system was suppressed. Is that all she was afraid of? Or as when her Dad was dying, sinking into a coma in the hospital room. Her brothers and sisters waited for her in the hospital conference room after he was pronounced dead to this world. She was delayed at a very long freight train crossing that morning. Could she have taken another route? Oh, but she wishes for that time now. She prays for it. She knows that she will have it upon her own death.

She knows now that she wants to make it easy for those left behind. She used to fear getting older, until she realized that *every single day is one more step closer to the unending joy of eternity. It matters not what ones age is now.*

She prays that all left will celebrate and be happy for her. There are so many different ways to prepare. There is so little time left; when maybe she should have been preparing all her life? One's life is a journey. Sometimes it is taken in carefully planned steps down the path, or sometimes in a relaxed ambling. It may even be in a rushed hectic run. Maybe 20 or 25 years on the outside-that's all the time she has left to do His work. Because of His suffering, she knows that she can move on without guilt, with deep repentance, for the time she has wasted. This is hard to recognize; more difficult to accept. Is this a false humility? She only deserves because she is made in His image, by her Creator. Nothing she did had anything to do with bringing about this most invaluable gift of Eternal Life. Satan wants her under condemnation. She relies on the word of God that tells her that there is no condemnation for the righteous. She received with gratitude His righteousness. She guards it.

> "It is only when we truly know and understand that we have a time on earth and that we have no way of knowing when our time is up that we will begin to live each day to the fullest, as if it were the only one we had."
>
> -Elizabeth Kubler-Ross

And so when she is dying, she would like to see her loved ones before she leaves them temporarily. She wants to be able to tell them again how much she loves them. She wants to tell them to always stay close to God, growing ever closer. Nothing else really matters. The Holy Spirit will comfort and counsel them always, no matter what they are facing in life. He will never leave them. She rests that she is leaving them in the good care of the Shepherd. She wants to tell them that she is rejoicing about seeing them in Heaven within a blink of an eye. She envisions them gathered round her; as she tells them good bye one final time in this world. She will be waiting for each in the next. She utters the prayer for them that she has prayed each morning, words that her Creator has reassured her with:

> "I make an everlasting covenant with them. I will never stop doing good to them; and I will inspire them to fear Me; so that they will never turn away from Me. I will rejoice in doing them good and will assuredly plant them in this land with all my heart and soul."

-The NLT Bible, Jeremiah 21:40-41

Her only response is "Hallelujah"! Thank You, my Father! That's all that is can be, Glory to Almighty God, her Father.

May her musings help each on his or her individual journey to find the Truth. May each spend time to find His joy, to ponder the greatness of this Gift. For now she continues her on her own pathway to help spread His kingdom to others. There seems so very much she wants to do, so many to see and talk with of Him. She anticipates, like a child waiting for the long awaited birthday gift, the greatest gift of all. For that is what she is hopes and prays for all.

And So She Thinks!

She ponders. She meditates. She thinks so much, about it all. The promises of healing realized, always, as He hears the prayers. The joy of relationships developed or restored, as time and effort is spent following her heart. Especially the relationship started, savored, built, and ever growing more deeply with her Savior, her God. She thinks about future relationships with, who are now unknown strangers to her. Perhaps the strangers she is yet to meet and love will be the action of such prayer. They are part of her purpose in being born. She wants to help her beloved country. America, in all of its beauty, as its facing challenges undaunted and yes, untrustingly, she prays. Perhaps the prayer, itself alone, is the action and answer.

She thinks more about the ending of her natural life. Death is the final victory and the final chapter in one's life. She knows now that there is another inconceivably longer time to live: eternity. It would be so foolish to think there is nothing after death; as silly as thinking there is no spirit world. Each chair, each table, each building, each bridge spanning wide rivers, each plane flying over oceans, each communication reaching around the globe in seconds is amazing. It is impossible not to realize that each of these that exist in this world began first, in the supernatural reality of someone's thoughts. Someone made in the image of God. She thanks the Holy Spirit of God for this insight, for this ability to believe. She spends her days of thinking simply:

Purpose

Near the log, fallen from the dead tree
Outside her bedroom window,
Partially hidden among the pines,
It quietly sits in the early filtered sunlight.
Unobtrusive in an unremarkable setting,
Yet powerful with a message.
It looks peaceful, patient, happy to be settled firmly,
Contentment: a pleasurable sense of completion.
While anxiously awaiting,
Today, tomorrow, many tomorrows.
An opportunity to worship like the fallen pine tree
Just being who she is, for her purpose.
No pretense, no disconnect,
No lack of goal or of provision;
Just peace…And love.

And so for now she creates her own reality in her mind based upon the promises of Christ's words. She knows now that this reality is a spiritual reality, which *was, is* and *will be ever present* now, from the beginning and into forever. Realizing that she must, concurrently, live in the natural reality of the world with all of it's' beauty and good, as well as all of it's' ugliness and evil. Her friends call her an "eternal optimist". This is the strategy for first of all, mapping out the destiny she desires, and then, to reach it, both in this world until the next. This is a true assessment of her attitude of happiness. It is her choice; as this is what she thinks about, for herself and for all. The Source of such optimism is to truly know and to believe Him, of saying yes to Him.

May each be blessed with this knowing and belief. May each come to know the depth of His love that is good and beautiful and carries one through any evil or ugliness. She bows in adoration and lifts her face and hands toward heaven in gratitude and praise. Hallelujah! Amen and Amen!

She truly does look forward to dying some day. Meanwhile, whatever comes her way, fun times or not so fun, no challenge will ever be insurmountable. Why? Simply spoken, she knows Him and trusts Him. She knows His word to be true and never changing. She accepts that she may not understand the whys and wherefores for evils, large and small, in this world. For it is by faith that she knows deeply that He will walk with her; at times even carry her if needed. How very blessed she is. She thanks Him constantly for all the wonderful things, tiny and huge. She thanks Him for His presence and His promises when things are difficult because she knows these, too, will pass. When she's in trouble she thanks Him for working it out for her. These events are only temporary. She loves to think about gifts of new mercy, grace, and understanding that are hers every day, just for the asking and receiving. Her words are inadequate to express her gratitude to her Savior.

Now, friends and unknown strangers alike, men, women and children, she asks each to think. Again, what is each thinking? It is one's choice which thoughts to let flutter right on by and which thoughts to keep forever. Each decides for herself or himself, after thinking about it. Free will is given exactly for that reason: to choose. As Calvin and Hobbes said, "We never have enough time to do *nothing*!" Sometimes doing nothing is the most valuable activity possible. For this is when she thinks. She guards what she thinks. She guards which thoughts to keep and which to not consider.

"Just like the winter, waiting for the sun again,I need You now."

"I Need You Now" in his album
"Your Grace Finds Me" Matt Redman.

Epilogue

She Now Thinks

She now thinks,
In a lighter tone, she walks with a lighter step.

In Spring, I wanna sing.
I wanna dance.
I wanna skip.
I wanna laugh.
I do!

In Summer, I wanna feel the grass
In my bare feet.
I wanna forever forget
About being neat.
I just wanna be free.
I am!

In Fall, want it all:
The sun,
The fun,
I love to run!

In Winter, a snowfall quiet,
A window brightly lit.
Friends, love, and peace,
Chocolate…
And no diet.
It goes so quick!

Afterward

Discussion Questions

Part I: S P R I N G

During this time of renewal, she thinks about and prays for healing.

Question I.A:

Which selection in this Part I of *She Thinks*! do you relate to? Why? Which pull at your emotions, causing you to think more about the issue presented? Is there a quote on these select pages that you would like think more about? What is it? What insight are you gaining?

Question I.B:

The author makes the statement that "She is well, because she thinks herself well." Do you think that this is possible? Why or why not? Consider medical brain and neurological research, accumulated over the last several years, about how our thoughts change the chemicals in our body, for good or bad.

Question II.C:

There are many more miracles; it seems, in other countries, especially in the Eastern Hemisphere. Do you think that's because in many ways citizens there, generation after generation, have been more "spiritual", always believing in some god, something beyond the natural, to explain their world? Is it somehow easier for them to believe then it is for us in the Western hemisphere? Or do you think it's because they do not have the medical care system that this country enjoys, wherein we have highly qualified doctors and hospital facilities at our fingertips? Are they more desperate? Here in the Western world, we are decidedly science and logic minded. "Show me", is the mantra; "then I will believe.

How does this thinking affect our faith for healing?

Part II: S U M M E R

She thinks about the beauty of full blossoming of flowers and of relationships.

Question II: A.

Have you had a "good friend", as described in this section? How do you recognize him/her a "good" friend? What qualities of a "good" friend are most important to you?

Question II: B:

Do you see yourself as a friend to others? Do you think it is hard work to be a "good" friend? Do you think that a friendship takes a long time to develop? Why or why not?

Question II.C:

Do we receive more than we give when we befriend another? Why is it hard for us to help our friends sometimes? Are the demands on our time worth shutting a friend out at times? Are some relationships toxic? What or where is the boundary between being a Christian, showing God's love, and stepping back from a relationship that you don't recognize as good for you? Where is the responsibility of love in such instances?

Part III: Autumn:

The Glorious Colors of our Country.

Part III.A:

What are your thoughts about the necessity of relaxing? What do you do to relax? Do you feel guilty when you take a day to relax, a half day, an hour?

Question III.B

Have you heard people tell you that you *must* be aware of events in the news? What does this mean to you? Can thinking about things beyond your control on a daily basis, especially if such events are negative, affect you negatively? Or are you allowing yourself to be out of touch of reality? How much news of today is too much?

Question III.C:

What is a reasonable amount of time to be spending alone with God, considering your daily schedule? Is it worth increasing? It is recognized that this time is often, if not always, the time for great spiritual growth. Is the result, the renewal, rebirth of your thinking, your spirit worth it to you? Do you agree that time alone with Him is the path to peace and joy? Or do you find that it can be sought and found other ways?

Question III.D:

Do you think it is more important to pray for our country everyday than it is to analyze what is going on continually? What is the difference? Why do you think so or not? How much is in your control? What are your options, as a citizen, of this great land? What are your options, as a Christian, to show His love to others who think differently from you? Who believe in a different god? Believing and trusting have an action waiting for you to ignite. What might that be?

Part IV: W I N T E R

A time of special beauty,
She thinks about how joyful death is
when considering eternity.

IV.A:

What is your idea as you think about death, premature or expected death?

IV.B:

Have you or someone close to you experienced the unexpected loss of a child? Is this different than the loss of an elderly parent or grandparent? How so? What occurs to you as you think about and relate two such experiences?

IV.C:

Is death of a loved one, the only traumatic loss that an individual can only experience? Can loss of a marriage relationship, career, or home all have a similar grieving processes? Are they similar or are they too different from the loss of a loved one to be compared?

Are there some losses that we must experience ourselves; that we truly cannot understand a friend's grief?

Endorsements from Readers

"You know in some books, even really good ones, you skip over a paragraph or two here or there, or sometimes over a page or two even. In this book I wanted to read *every single word*. I didn't want to skip over even one." -G.L.S.

"Your book touched me deeply. The skill with which you use words was like hearing a symphony being created. It caused me to stop, ponder and think. As I listened my spirit was stirred as I was actually hearing notes created from the sounds of heaven."-J.A..S.

"Use the part about my son if it will help someone."-B.J.C.

"It made me grateful for the privilege of having you in our lives. You have run an amazing race of faith!-E. & E.G.

"You have the heart of God and I feel each beat. The writing on loss; May it help myself and others to leave it all at the feet of our God."-C.R.S.

"The part about the fear of cancer returning was wow; I could hardly read it". –R.V.

"Better than best sellers I've read."-R.F.

"You captured what I feel, that I could not put into words. No one understands. You took me farther."-T.N.

From a friend, this poem:

Words of the Heart

Words on a page
Written by a friend,
Much more than words
Pieces of each heart.
Thoughts of the mind,
Agony of the soul
Peace of the spirit
Love of the Father.
Joy never ending,
Faith increasing.
Reality of eternity,
Life eternal.
No pain
No tears
No heartache.
Love forevermore.

-Carole R. Storteboom, 2013

Sources

Sacred Texts:

The Prayer Bible New Living Translation, Tyndale House Publishers. Wheaton, Illinois. 2003. Syswerda, Jean E., General Editor

The Quest Study Bible New International Version, Revised. Grand Rapids, Michigan: 2003

Books

Batterson, Mark, *Be A Circle Maker*. Zondervan Publishers. Grand Rapids, MI.

Batterson, Mark, *The Circle Maker*. Zondervan Publishers. Grand Rapids, MI

Berry, Carmen Renee & Traeder, Tamara, *Girlfriends, Invisible Bonds Enduring Ties*. Wildcat Canyon Press, a division of Circulus Publishing Group, Inc. 1995.Berkeley, CA

Booher, Dianna, *Fresh Cut flowers for A Friend*. .Countryman Publishers, a division of Thomas Nelson, Incl. 2002 Nashville, Tenn.

Browning, Elizabeth Barrett (1806-1861) American/English poet of Victorian era.

Cage, John (1942-1992) quote from "Where Are We Going And What Are We Doing?' from ...*And Wisdom Comes Quietly* A Helen Exley Gift book. Exley Publications. 2000. N.Y., N.Y. un-numbered pages.

Calvin and Hobbes comic strip character created by Bill Waterson. Calvin and Hobbes are imaginary humorist/philosophers. Several books written between. 1987-2005. Quotes herein taken from *The Authoritative Calvin and Hobbes*. p.213.

Camus, Albert (1913-1960) French Nobel prize winning author, journalist and philosopher.

Chinese Proverb found in ....*And Wisdom Comes Quietly*. A Helen Exley Gift book, Exley Publications. 2000. N.Y., N.Y.

Dickenson, Emily (1830-1886) American poet.

Emerson, Ralph Waldo (1803-1882) American essayist, poet, lecturer.

Huxley, Aldus (1894-1963) English writer, humanist, pacifist, and satirist. On line site: Wikipedia

Leaf, Caroline. *Who Switched Off My Brain? Controlling Toxic Thoughts and Emotions*. Published by Improv Ltd.Publishers. Distributed by Thomas Nelson Publishers. 2009

Lewis, C.S. (1888-1963) Irish novelist and poet. Well known works include but are not limited to *Chronicles of Narnia*, and *Space Trilogy*. Awesome C.S. Lewis Quotes by Josh Wiley. "What Christians Want To Know" found on internet Oct., 2011

Montaigne, Michel de (1533-1592) Influential writer of French renaissance period.

Radner, Gilda (1948-1969) American comedienne and author of *It's Always Something,* an extraordinary autobiography. Gilda left a legacy in diagnostic center built and Gilda's Clubs, an international network of places that give support to cancer victims and their families.

Ross, Elizabeth K. (1926-2004) American journalist and social researcher. Well known works includes but are not limited to *On Death and Dying.*

Tolkien, J.R.R. (1892-1973) English author, academic, and poet. Well known works include but are not limited to *The Hobbit, Lord of the Rings,* and *Beowulf*

Scholma, Vicki., *Above The Valley.* Tate Publishing and Enterprises, LLC. Oklahoma. 2014.

Musical Lyrics

"Come Saturday Morning" written by Fred Karlin (music) and Dory Previn (lyrics).1970 Recorded originally by the Sandpipers from the Sterile Cuckoo album.

22. "I Need You Now", Matt Redman from album "Your Grace Finds Me"

Poetry

All poetry, free form or stanza, was written by author, *unless otherwise noted and source identified.*

Printed in the United States
By Bookmasters